MOM'S DIARY

THE FIRST TWO YEARS

YUL KIM

WESTBOW
PRESS®
A DIVISION OF THOMAS NELSON
& ZONDERVAN

WestBow Press books may be ordered through booksellers or by contacting:

WestBow Press
A Division of Thomas Nelson & Zondervan
1663 Liberty Drive
Bloomington, IN 47403
www.westbowpress.com
1 (866) 928-1240

ISBN: 978-1-5127-9198-3 (sc)
ISBN: 978-1-5127-9199-0 (e)

Library of Congress Control Number: 2017909644

Print information available on the last page.

WestBow Press rev. date: 08/15/2017

ACKNOWLEDGMENTS

Without their help and support, this book would not have been fulfilled.

God, who gave me the enthusiasm to draw.

My forever cowalker, my husband, Tae.

The source of all the ideas for this book, my son, Sion.

My mental supporters, my parents, Kitae and Sookhyun, and my sister, Lynn.

All my friends and coworkers who encouraged me to finish and publish this book, especially Leigh, Heather, and Moo Kyung.

NEW WORKOUT ROUTINE

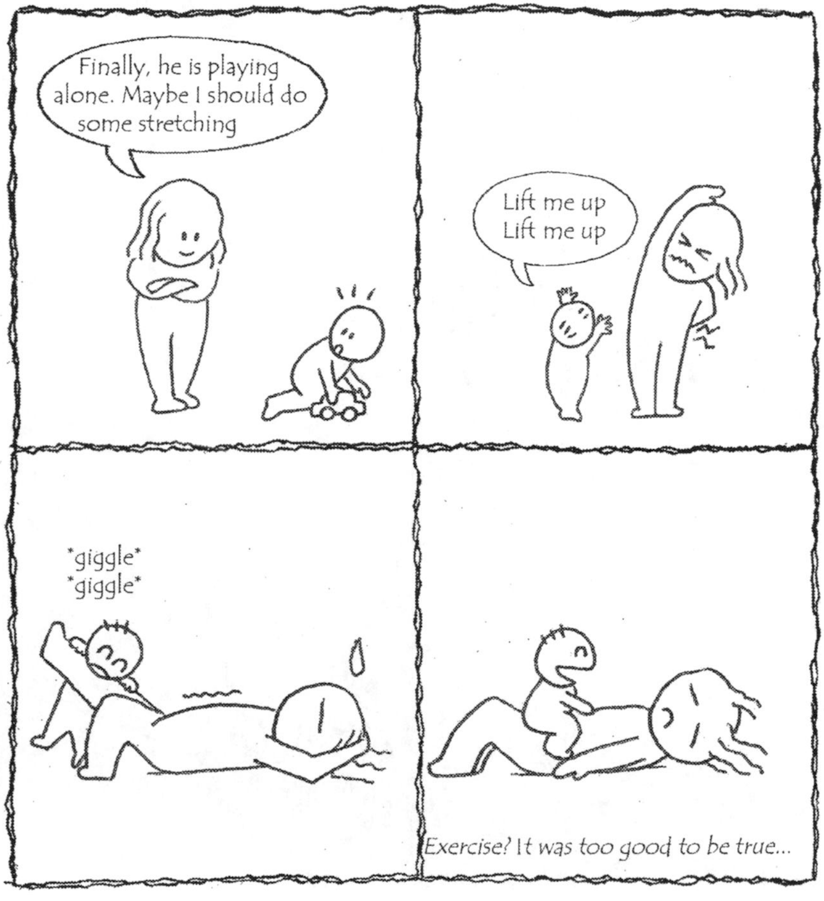
Finally, he is playing alone. Maybe I should do some stretching
Lift me up
Lift me up
giggle
giggle
Exercise? It was too good to be true...

TRAITOR

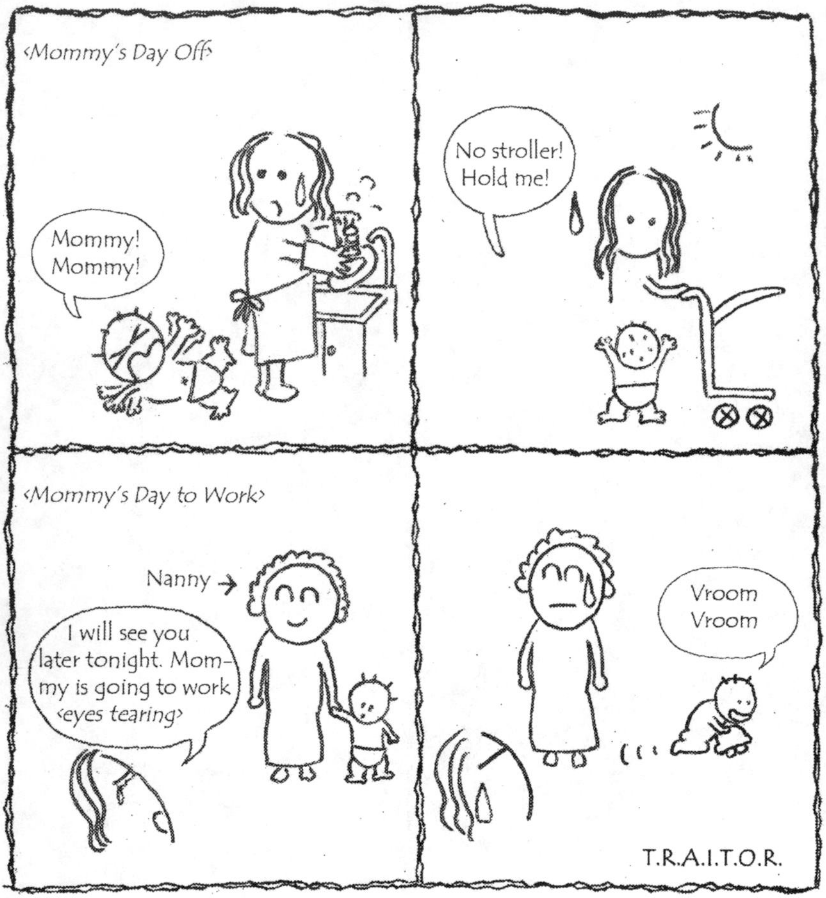
<Mommy's Day Off>
Mommy! Mommy!
No stroller! Hold me!
<Mommy's Day to Work>
Nanny →
I will see you later tonight. Mommy is going to work <eyes tearing>
Vroom Vroom
T.R.A.I.T.O.R.

JUST LIKE MOMMY

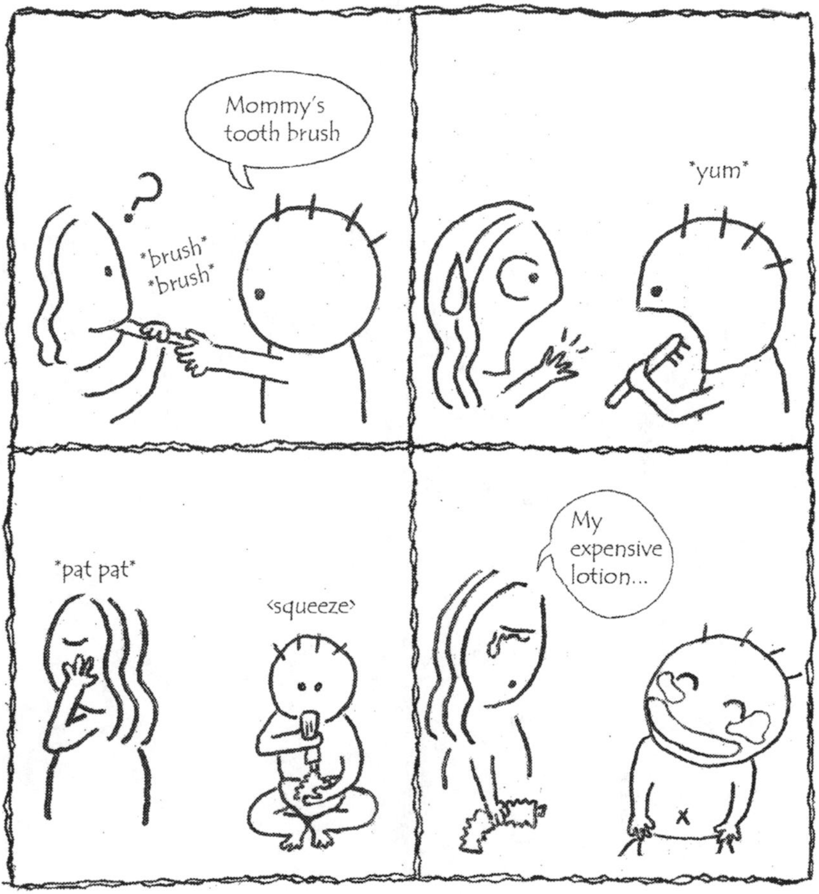

Mommy's tooth brush
brush *brush*
yum
pat pat
‹squeeze›
My expensive lotion...

TURN OF EVENTS

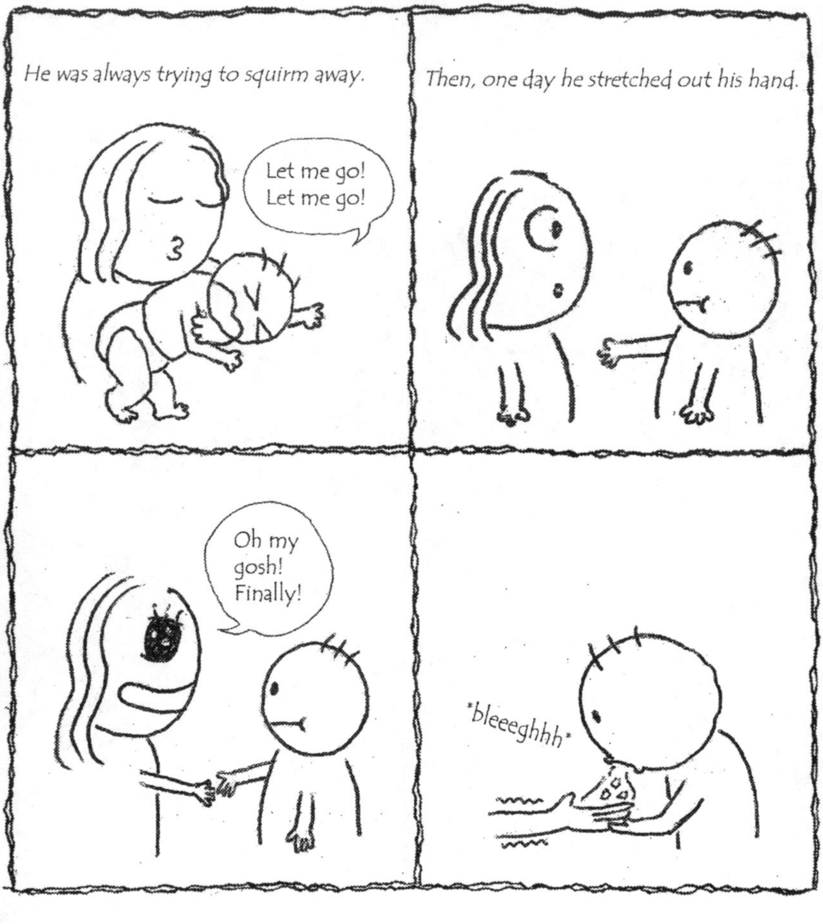
He was always trying to squirm away.
Let me go! Let me go!
Then, one day he stretched out his hand.
Oh my gosh! Finally!
bleeeghhh

SHY BABY

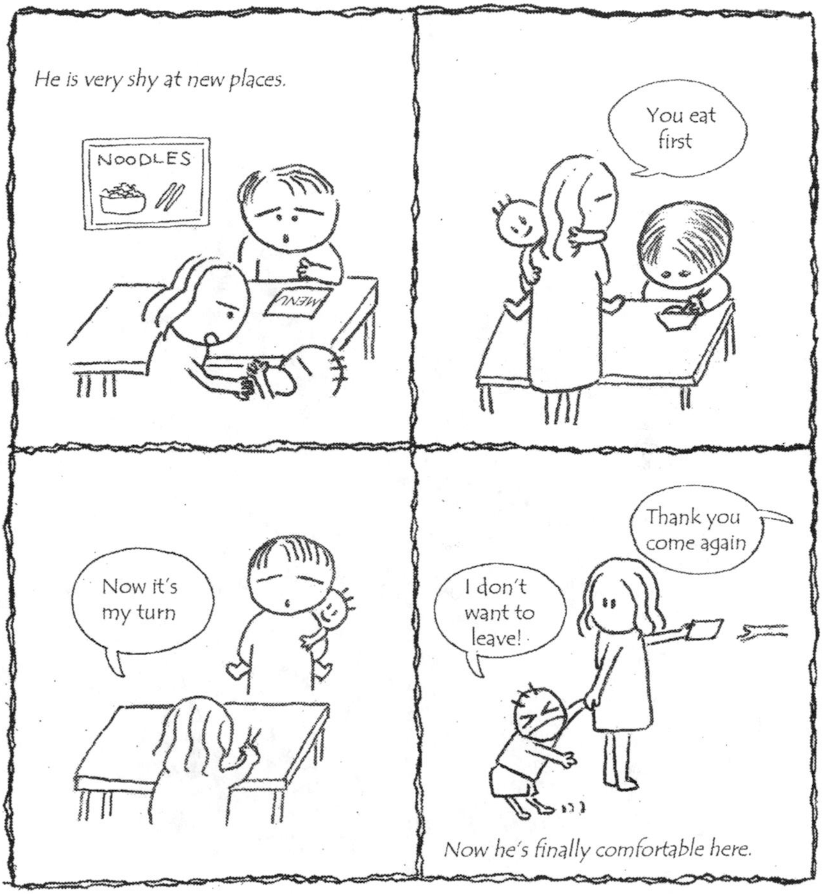
He is very shy at new places.
NOODLES
MENU
You eat first
Now it's my turn
Thank you come again
I don't want to leave!
Now he's finally comfortable here.

MOMMY'S IMAGINATION

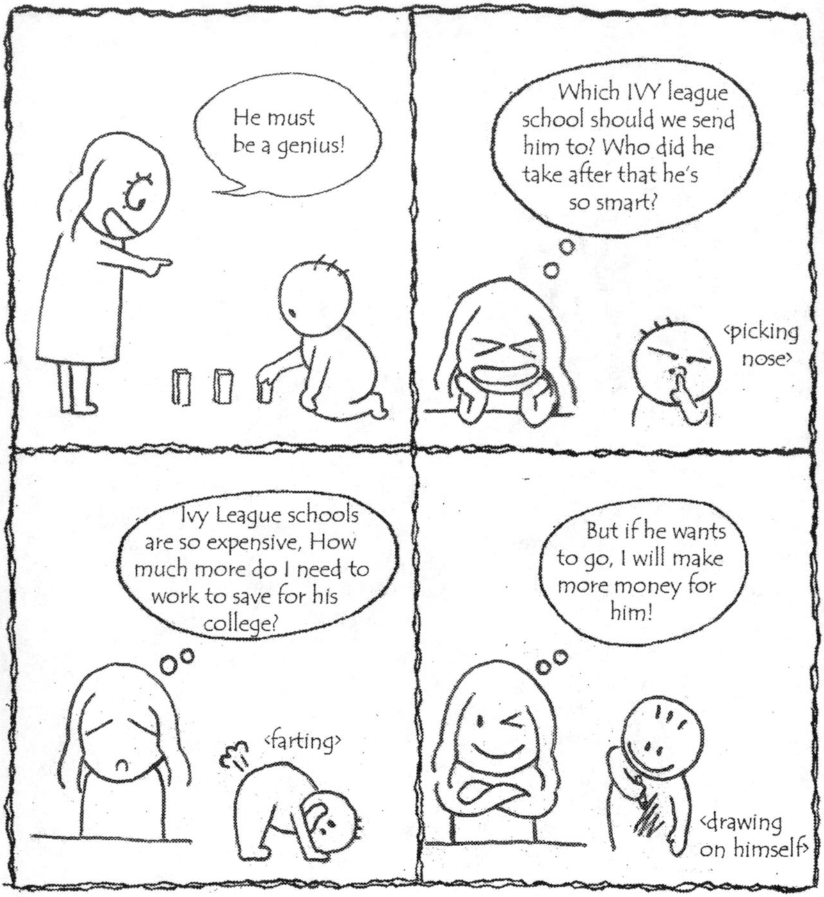
He must be a genius!
Which IVY league school should we send him to? Who did he take after that he's so smart?
<picking nose>
Ivy League schools are so expensive, How much more do I need to work to save for his college?
<farting>
But if he wants to go, I will make more money for him!
<drawing on himself>

MOMMY, THE HEALER

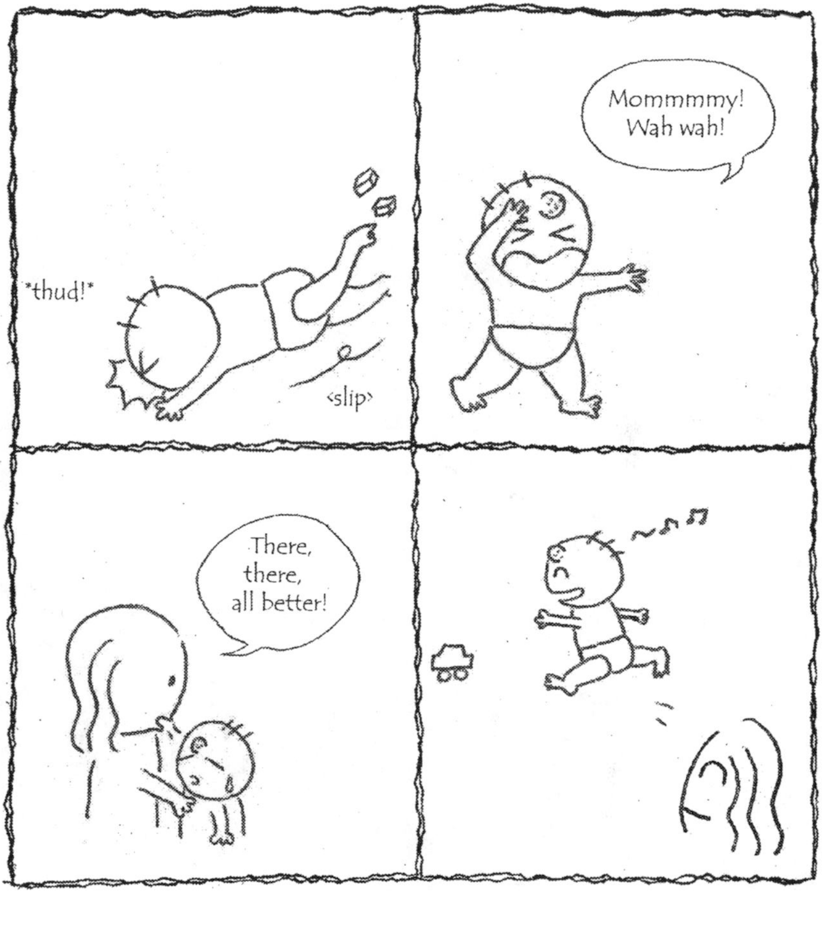

thud!
‹slip›
Mommmmy! Wah wah!
There, there, all better!

HIS NAP TIME IS MY REST TIME

WHAT A RELIEF!

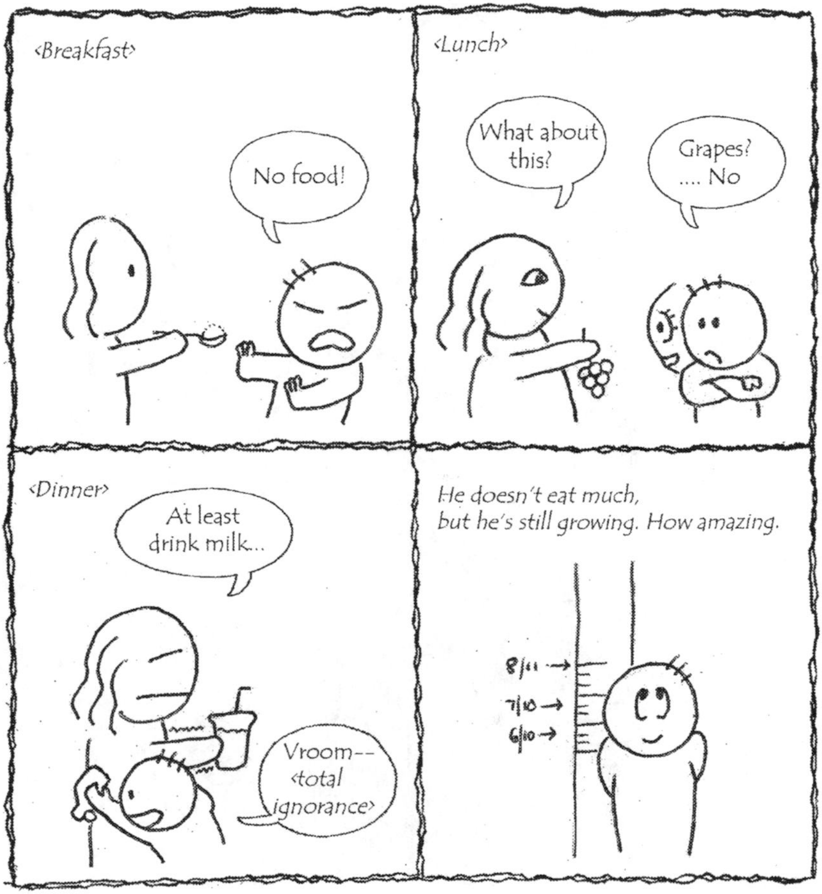

<Breakfast>
No food!
<Lunch>
What about this?
Grapes? .... No
<Dinner>
At least drink milk...
Vroom-- <total ignorance>
He doesn't eat much, but he's still growing. How amazing.

KISSING MACHINE

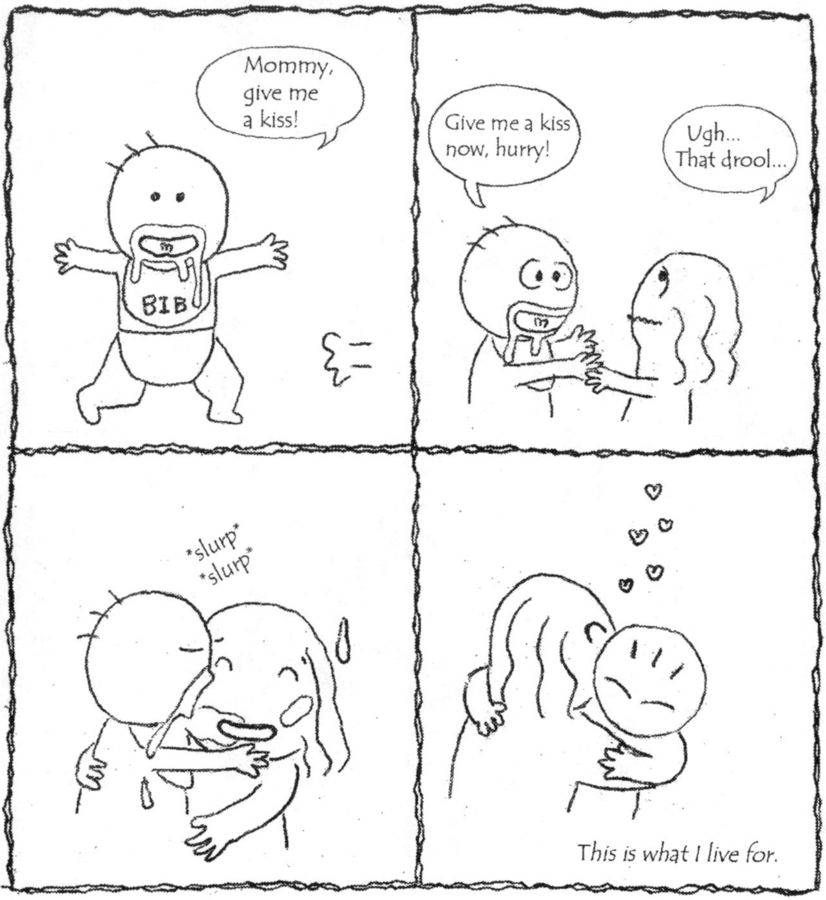
Mommy, give me a kiss!
BIB
Give me a kiss now, hurry!
Ugh... That drool...
slurp *slurp*
This is what I live for.

TWO-FACED

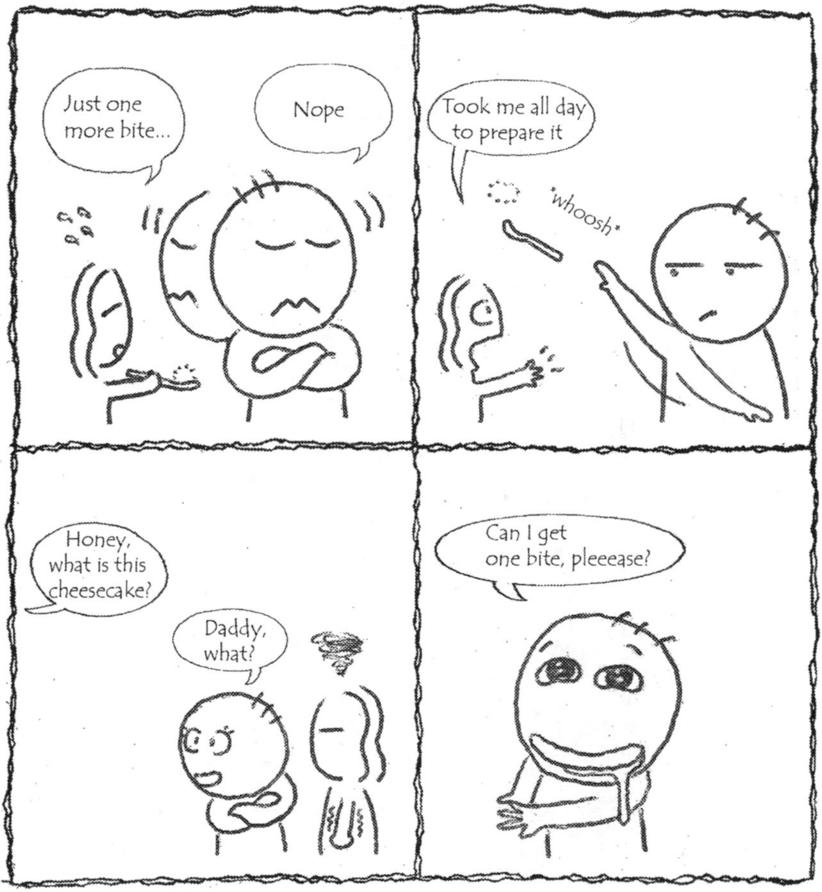
Just one more bite...
Nope
Took me all day to prepare it
whoosh
Honey, what is this cheesecake?
Daddy, what?
Can I get one bite, pleeease?

THE POWER OF PIZZA

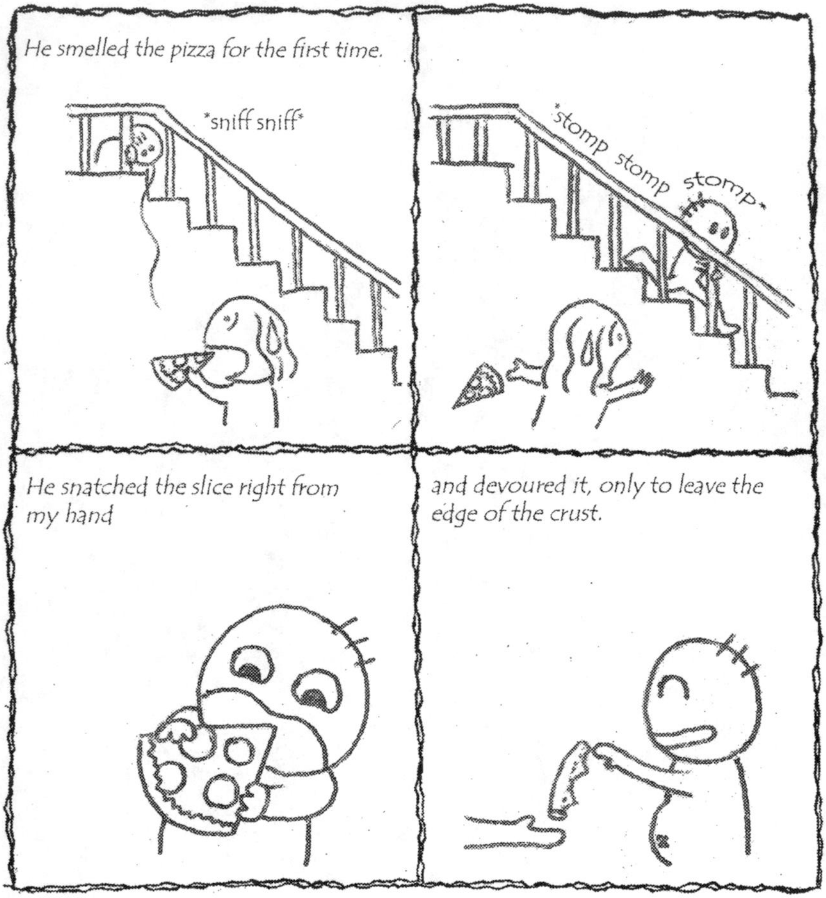
He smelled the pizza for the first time.
sniff sniff
stomp stomp stomp
He snatched the slice right from my hand
and devoured it, only to leave the edge of the crust.

CONFIDENCE

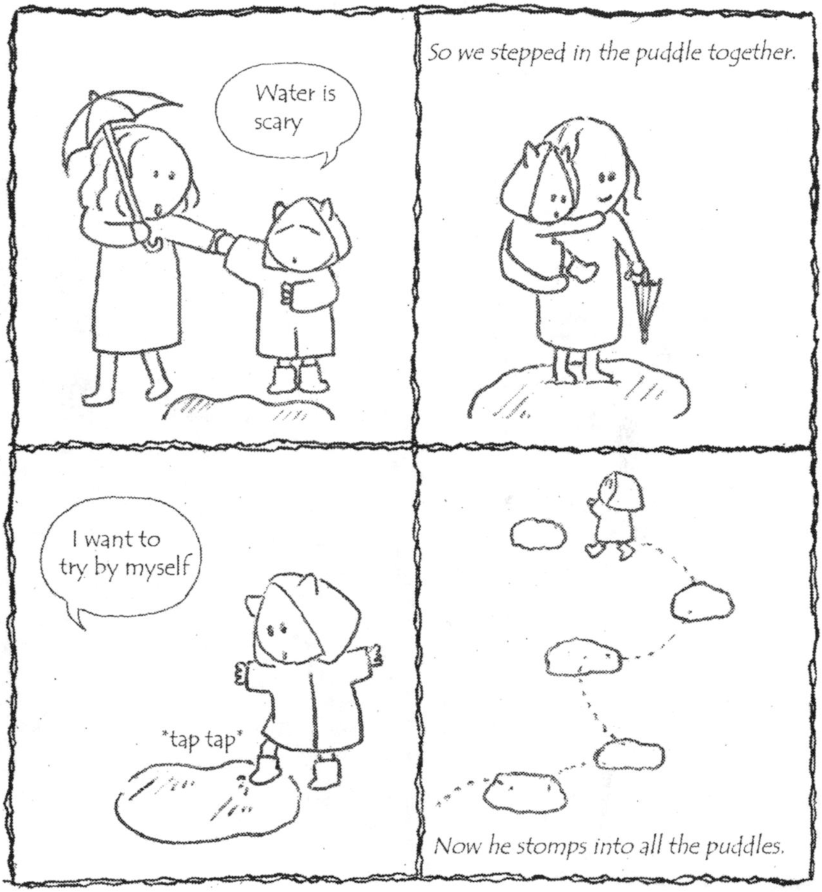
Water is scary
So we stepped in the puddle together.
I want to try by myself
tap tap
Now he stomps into all the puddles.

ONLY A MOM CAN ENDURE

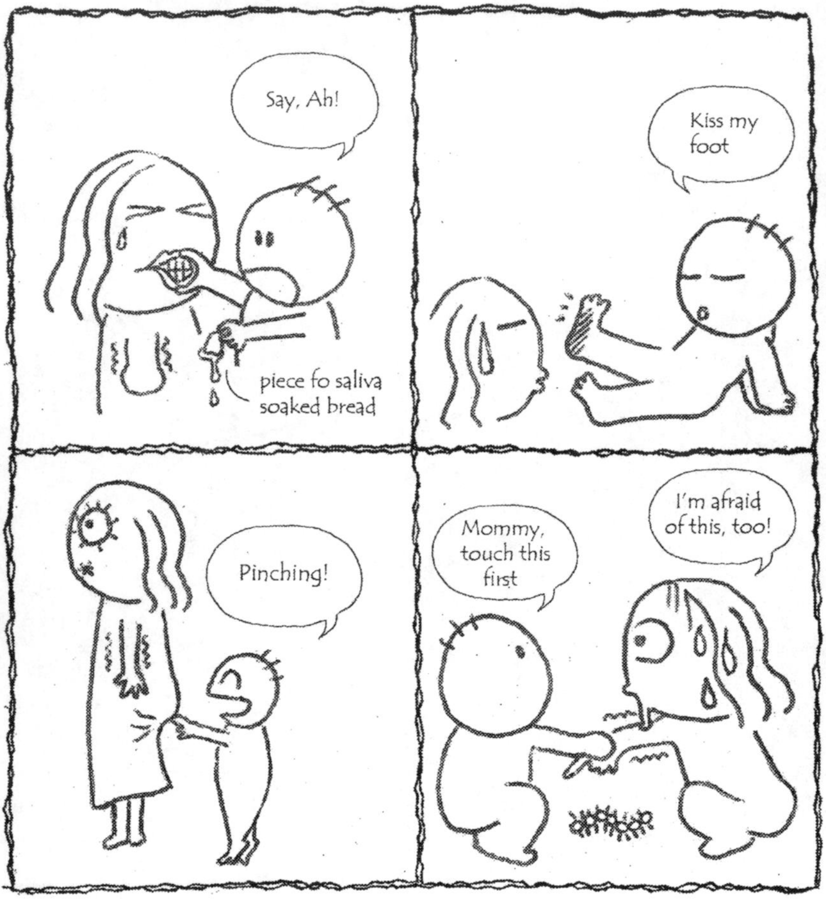

Say, Ah!
piece fo saliva soaked bread
Kiss my foot
Pinching!
Mommy, touch this first
I'm afraid of this, too!

FOREVER WITH MOMMY

He just wanted my company.

FIRST SOCIAL SKILLS

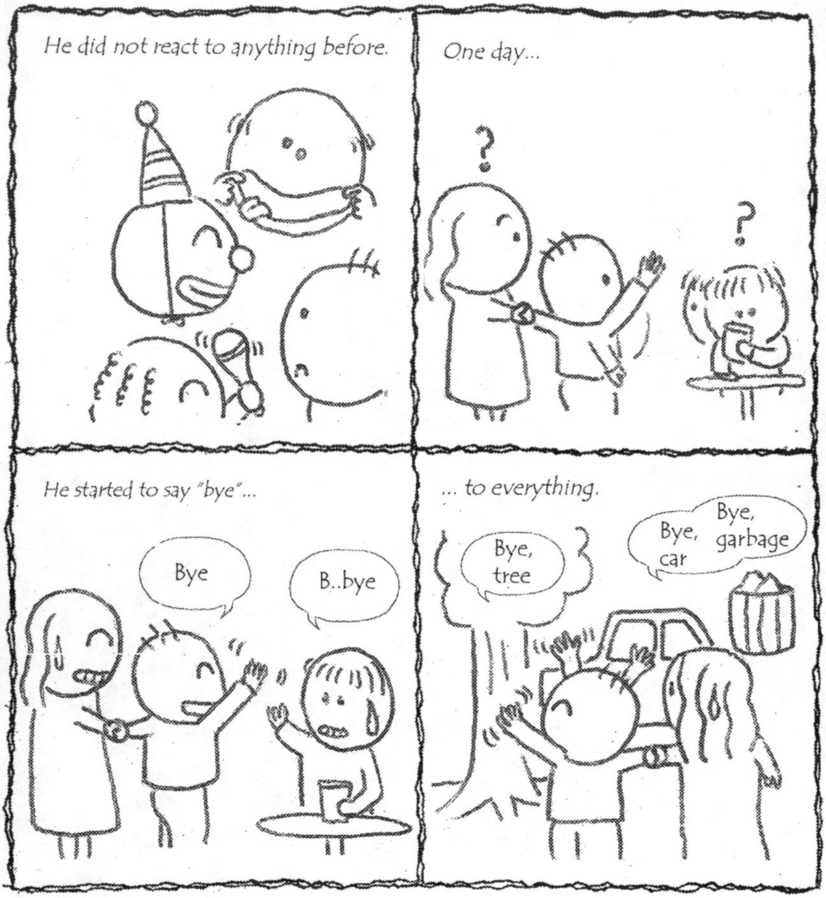
He did not react to anything before.
One day...
?
?
He started to say "bye"...
Bye
B..bye
... to everything.
Bye, tree
Bye, car
Bye, garbage

ASSOCIATION

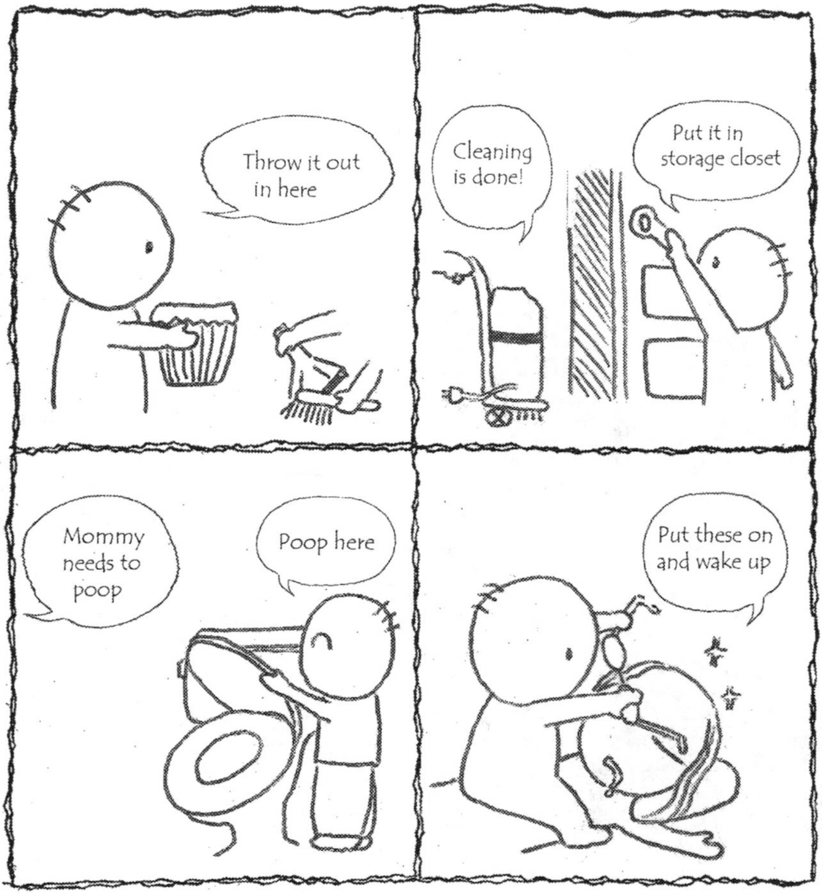
Throw it out in here
Cleaning is done!
Put it in storage closet
Mommy needs to poop
Poop here
Put these on and wake up

IMAGINATION

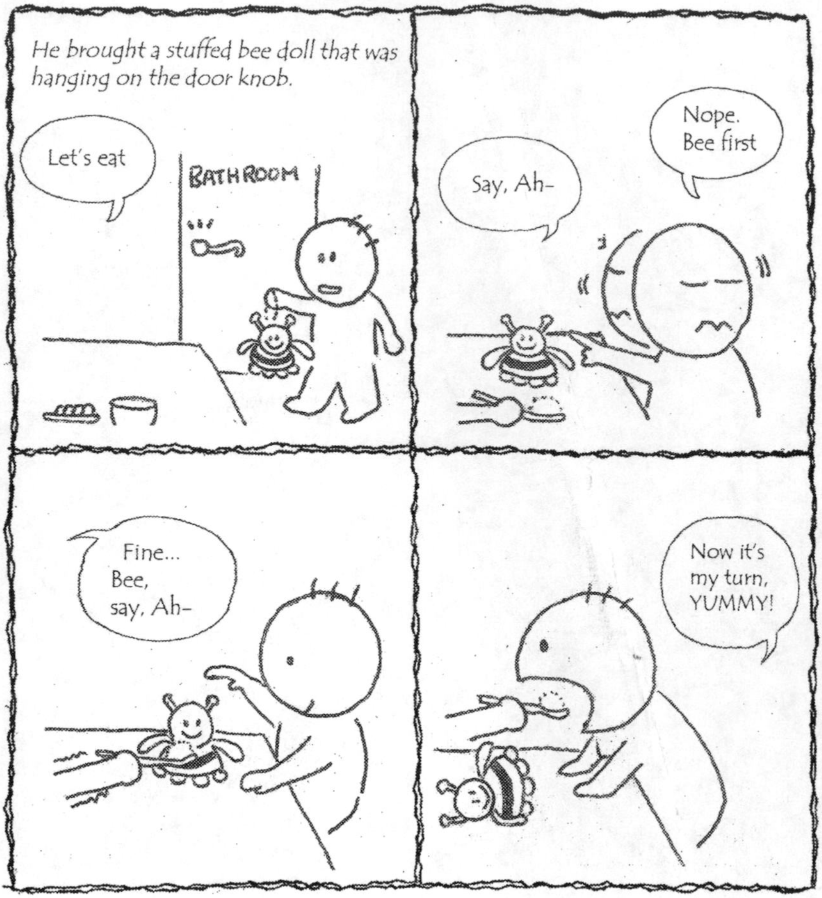

He brought a stuffed bee doll that was hanging on the door knob.
Let's eat
BATHROOM
Say, Ah-
Nope. Bee first
Fine... Bee, say, Ah-
Now it's my turn, YUMMY!

BEDTIME RITUAL

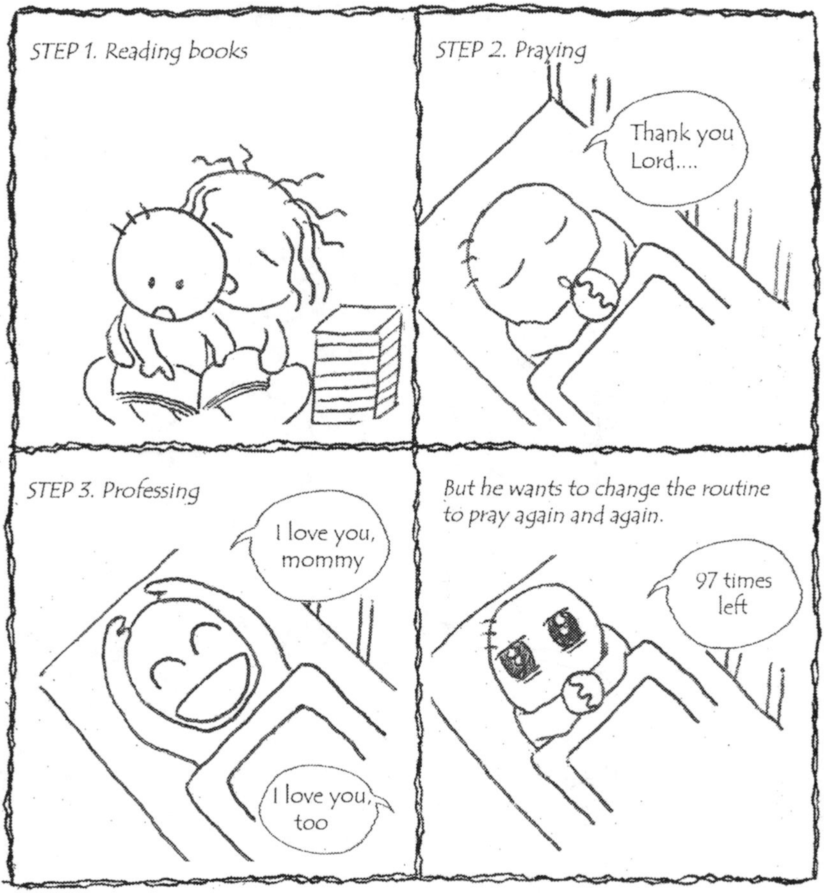
STEP 1. Reading books
STEP 2. Praying
Thank you Lord....
STEP 3. Professing
I love you, mommy
I love you, too
But he wants to change the routine to pray again and again.
97 times left

A CLAIRVOYANT

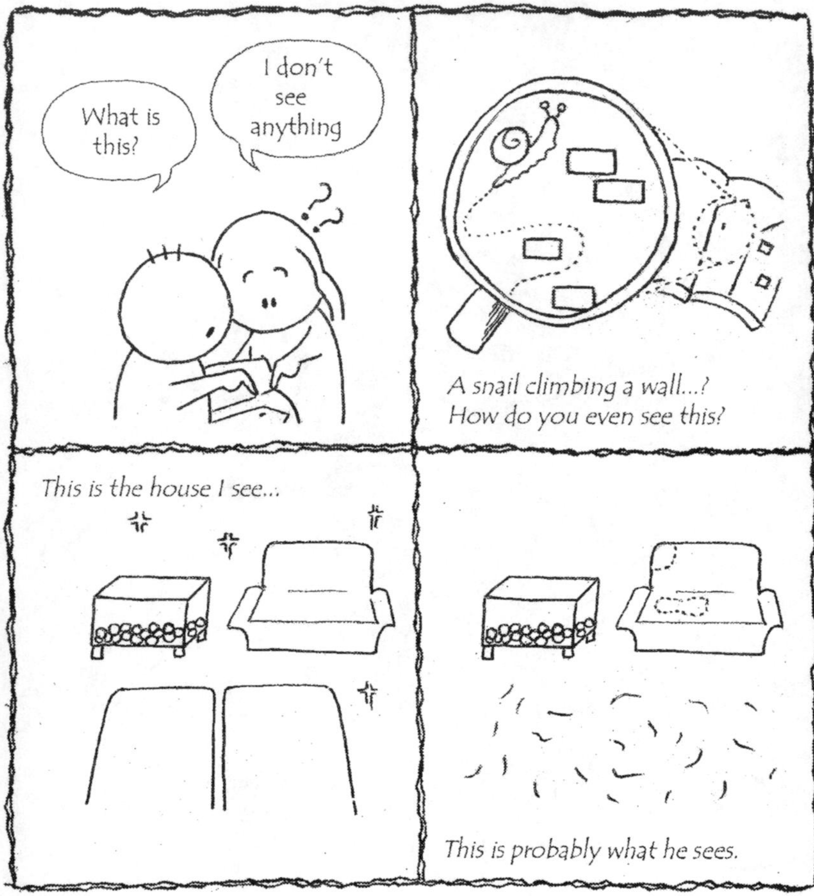
What is this?
I don't see anything
A snail climbing a wall...?
How do you even see this?
This is the house I see...
This is probably what he sees.

IT'S ALL ABOUT TIMING

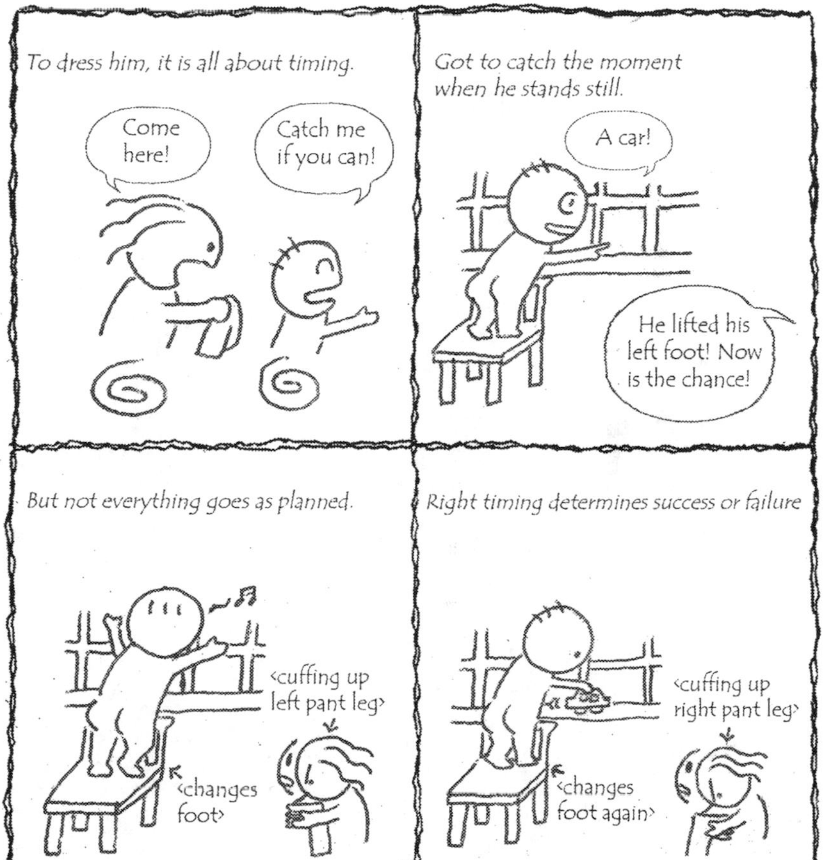

To dress him, it is all about timing.
Come here!
Catch me if you can!
Got to catch the moment when he stands still.
A car!
He lifted his left foot! Now is the chance!
But not everything goes as planned.
‹cuffing up left pant leg›
‹changes foot›
Right timing determines success or failure
‹cuffing up right pant leg›
‹changes foot again›

CHOOSE YOUR WORDS WISELY

GETTING ATTENTION

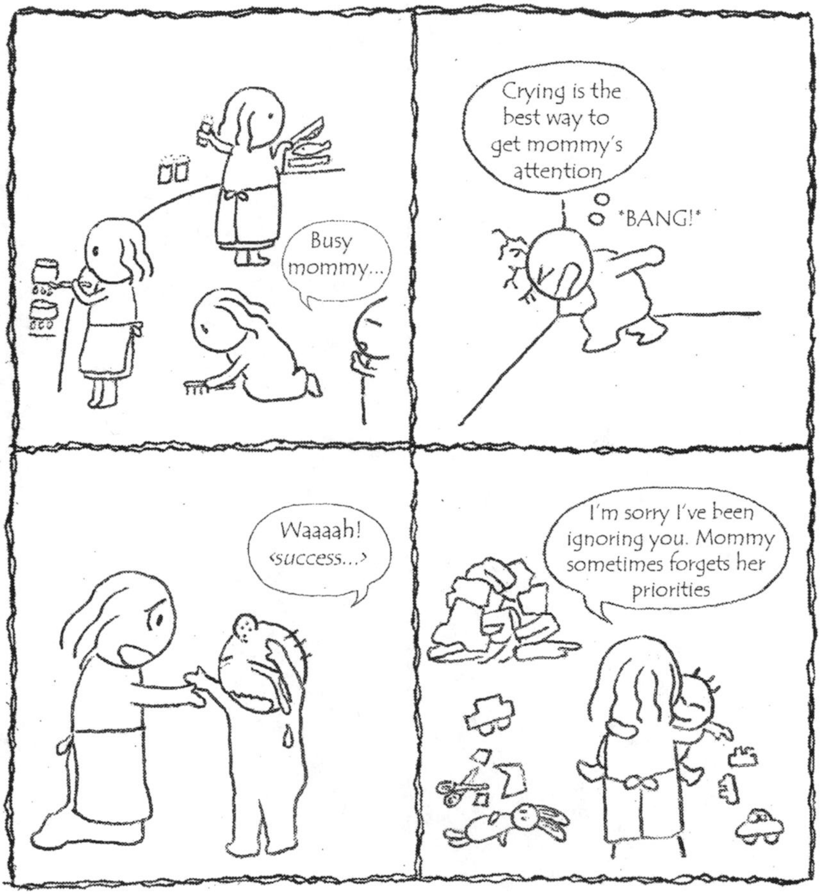
Busy mommy...
Crying is the best way to get mommy's attention
BANG!
Waaaah! ‹success...›
I'm sorry I've been ignoring you. Mommy sometimes forgets her priorities

COMPLIMENT #1

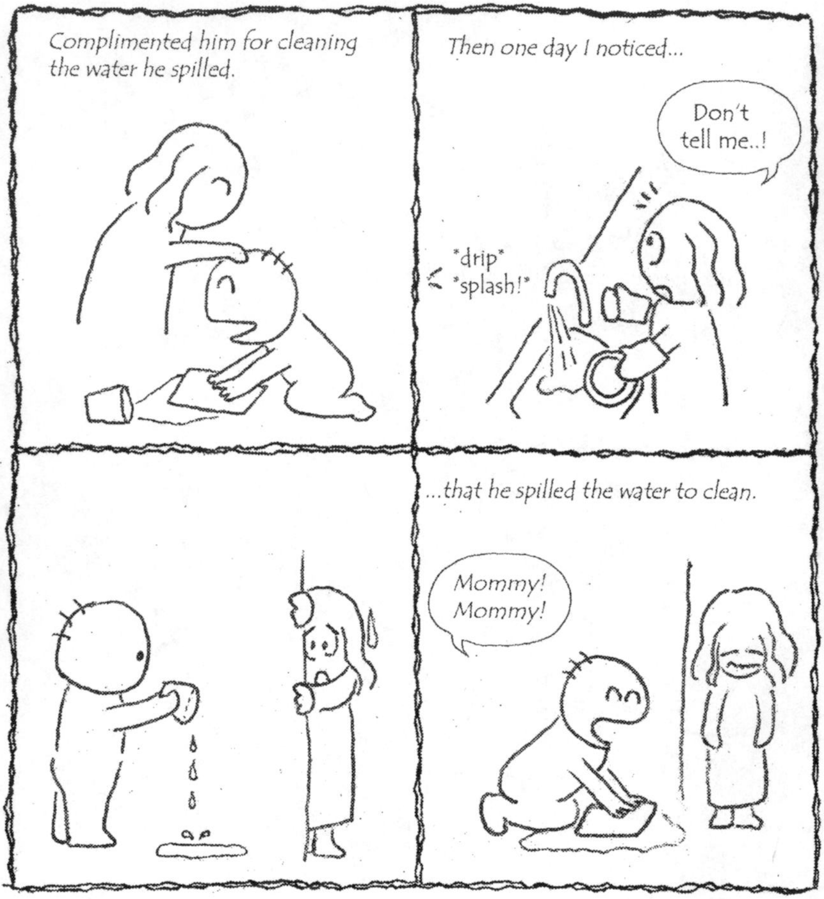
Complimented him for cleaning the water he spilled.
Then one day I noticed...
Don't tell me..!
drip *splash!*
...that he spilled the water to clean.
Mommy! Mommy!

WISHFUL THINKING ...

In the crib, he was at 1 month old

at 6 months old

at 2 years old

He will be this big soon...
Don't grow too fast, my precious!

BRUISES

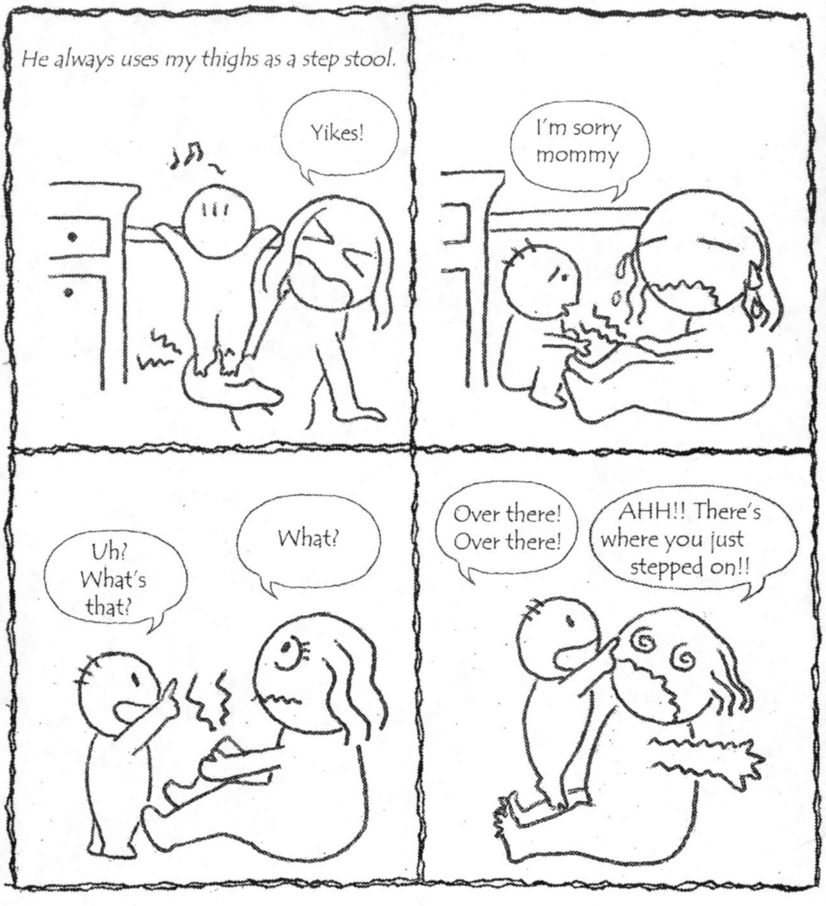

He always uses my thighs as a step stool.
Yikes!
I'm sorry mommy
Uh? What's that?
What?
Over there! Over there!
AHH!! There's where you just stepped on!!

SECURE NEXT TO MOMMY

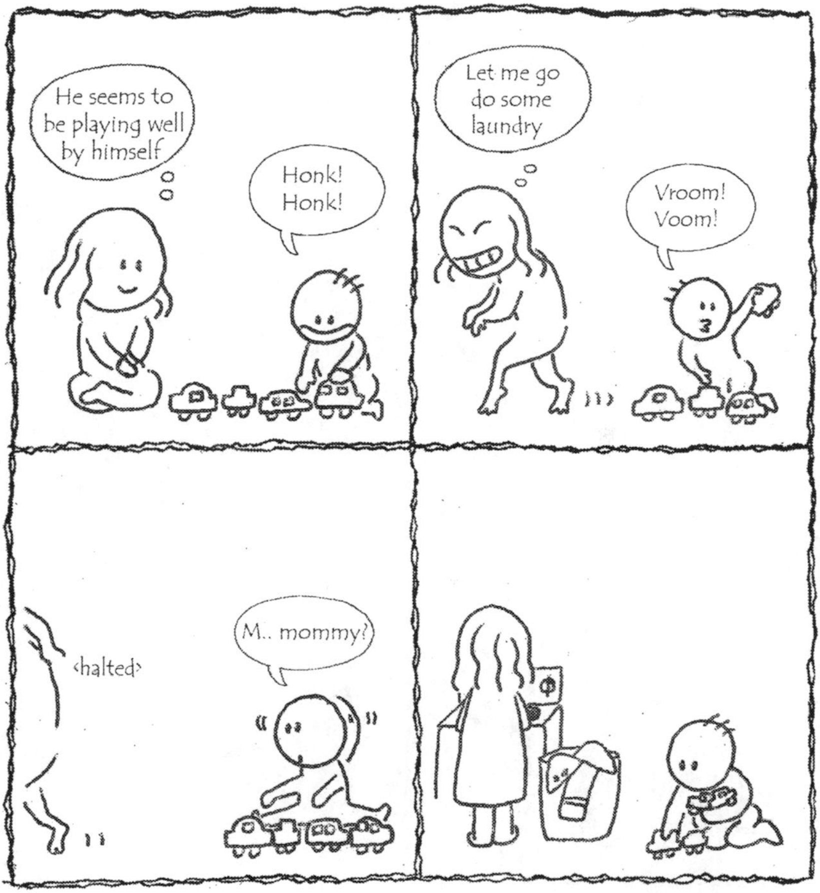
He seems to be playing well by himself
Honk! Honk!
Let me go do some laundry
Vroom! Voom!
<halted>
M.. mommy?

CLEANING

He pulled out sheets of baby wipe,

wiped here and there,

then came near to me...

to also clean my eye glasses.

squeak
squeak

BRAVEHEART

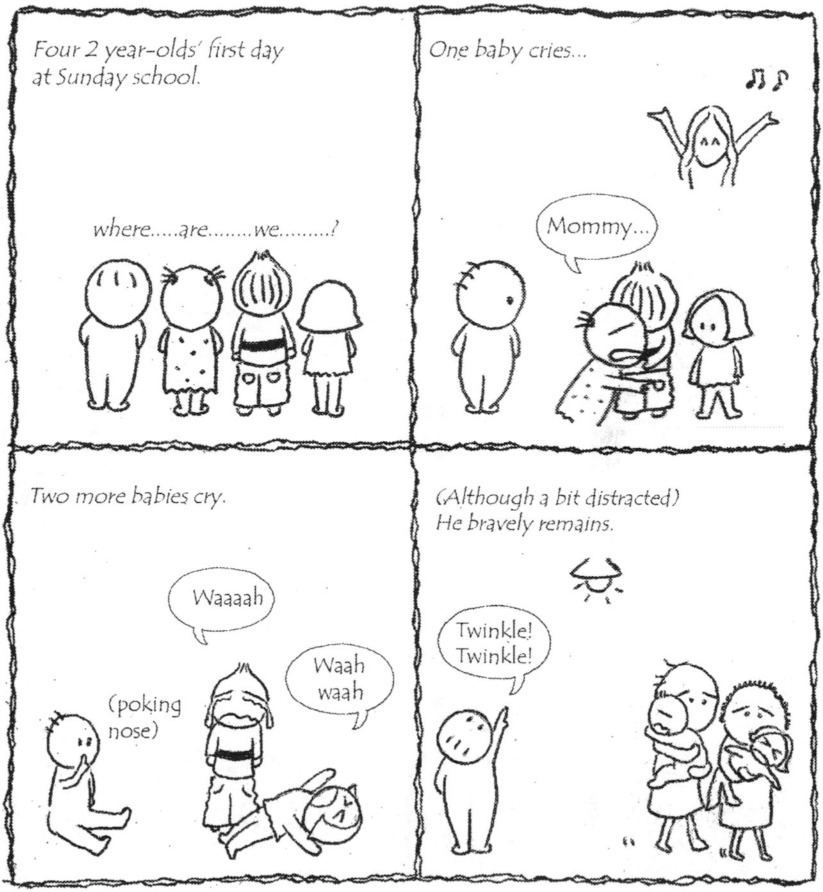
Four 2 year-olds' first day at Sunday school.
where.....are........we.........?
One baby cries...
Mommy...
Two more babies cry.
Waaaah
Waah waah
(poking nose)
(Although a bit distracted) He bravely remains.
Twinkle! Twinkle!

IT'S YOUR FAULT

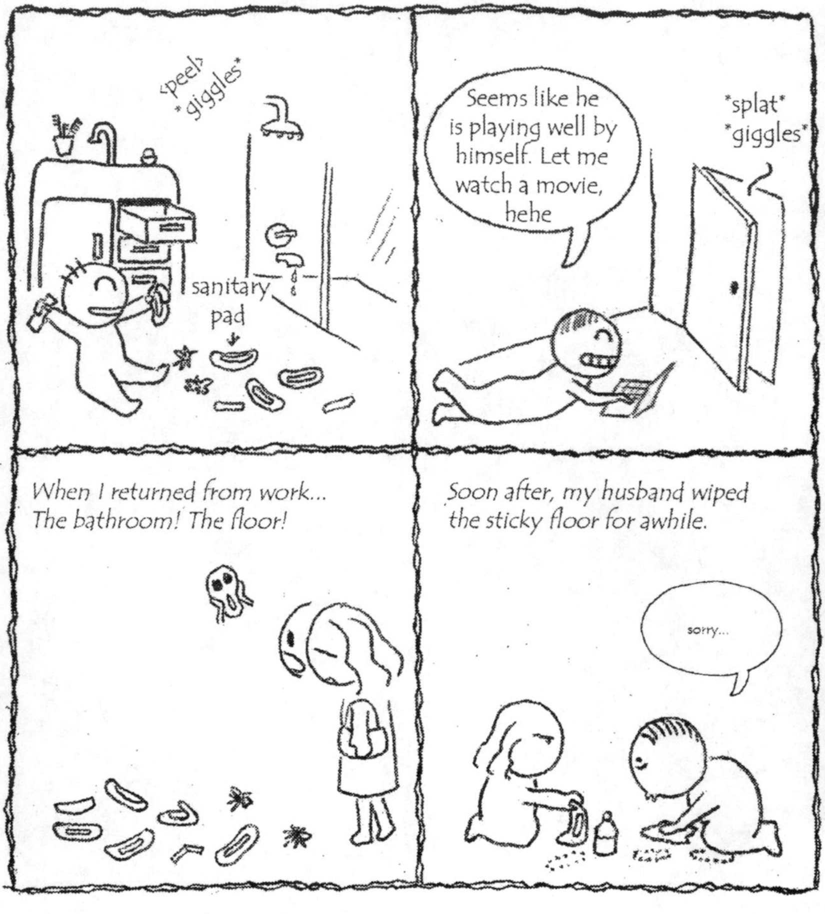

‹peel›
giggles
sanitary pad
Seems like he is playing well by himself. Let me watch a movie, hehe
splat
giggles
When I returned from work...
The bathroom! The floor!
Soon after, my husband wiped the sticky floor for awhile.
sorry...

BATTERY CHARGER

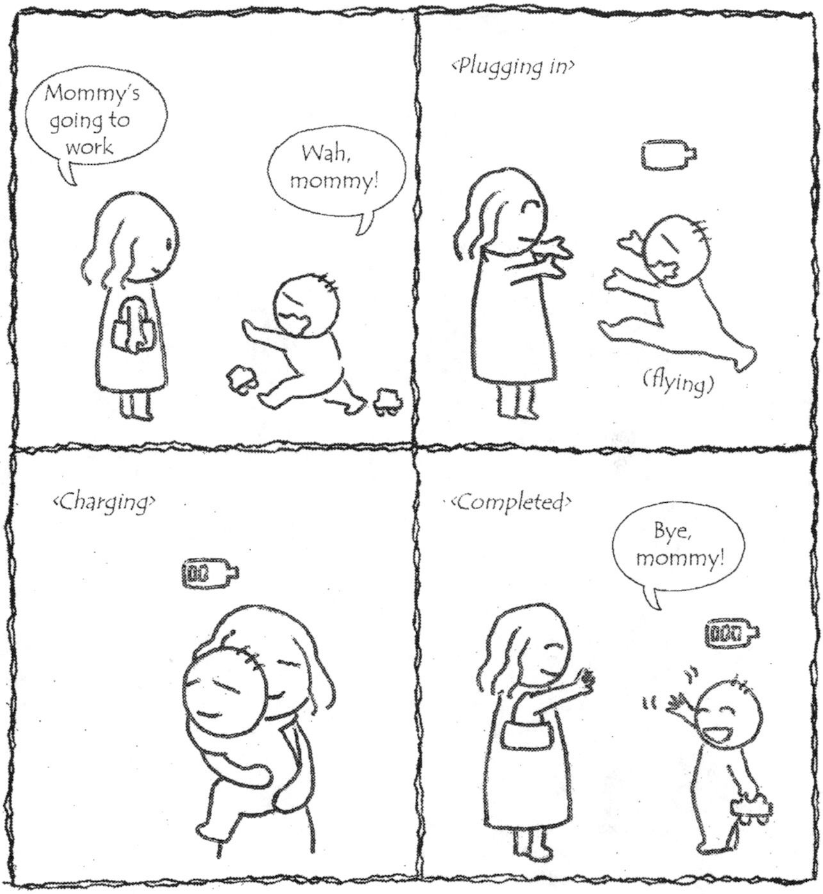
Mommy's going to work
Wah, mommy!
<Plugging in>
(flying)
<Charging>
<Completed>
Bye, mommy!

DIET

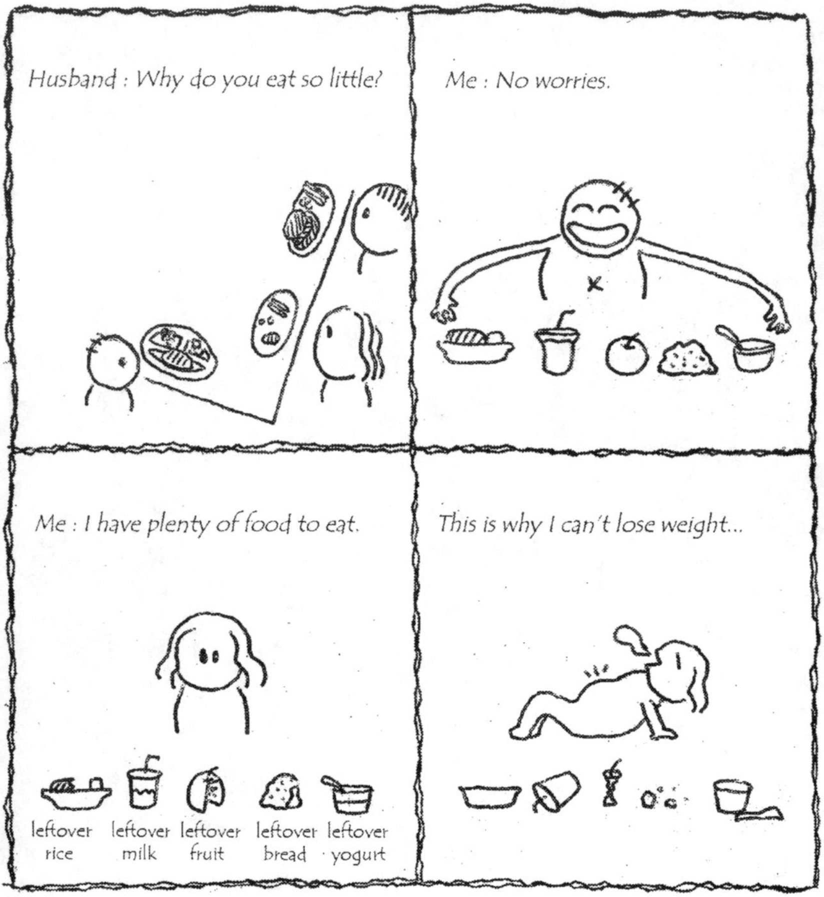
Husband : Why do you eat so little?
Me : No worries.
Me : I have plenty of food to eat.
leftover rice
leftover milk
leftover fruit
leftover bread
leftover yogurt
This is why I can't lose weight...

ENDLESS IMAGINATION

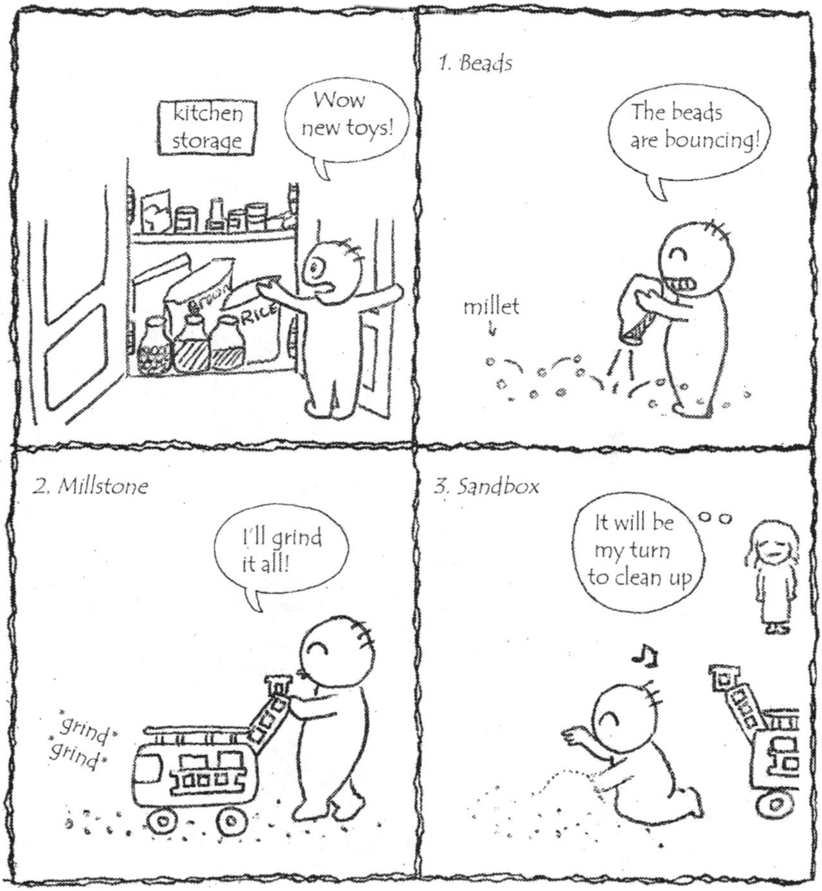
kitchen storage
Wow new toys!
RICE
1. Beads
The beads are bouncing!
millet
2. Millstone
I'll grind it all!
grind
grind
3. Sandbox
It will be my turn to clean up

DON'T FORGET ME, MOMMY

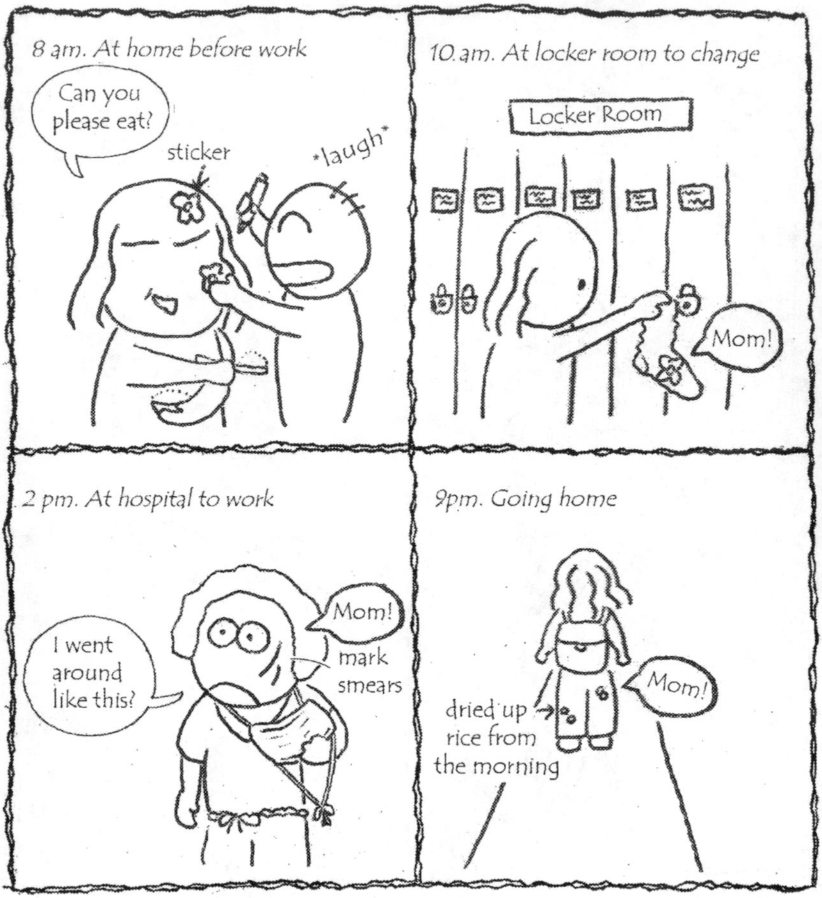
8 am. At home before work
Can you please eat?
sticker
laugh
10.am. At locker room to change
Locker Room
Mom!
2 pm. At hospital to work
I went around like this?
Mom!
mark smears
9pm. Going home
Mom!
dried up rice from the morning

MORNING ASSIGNMENT

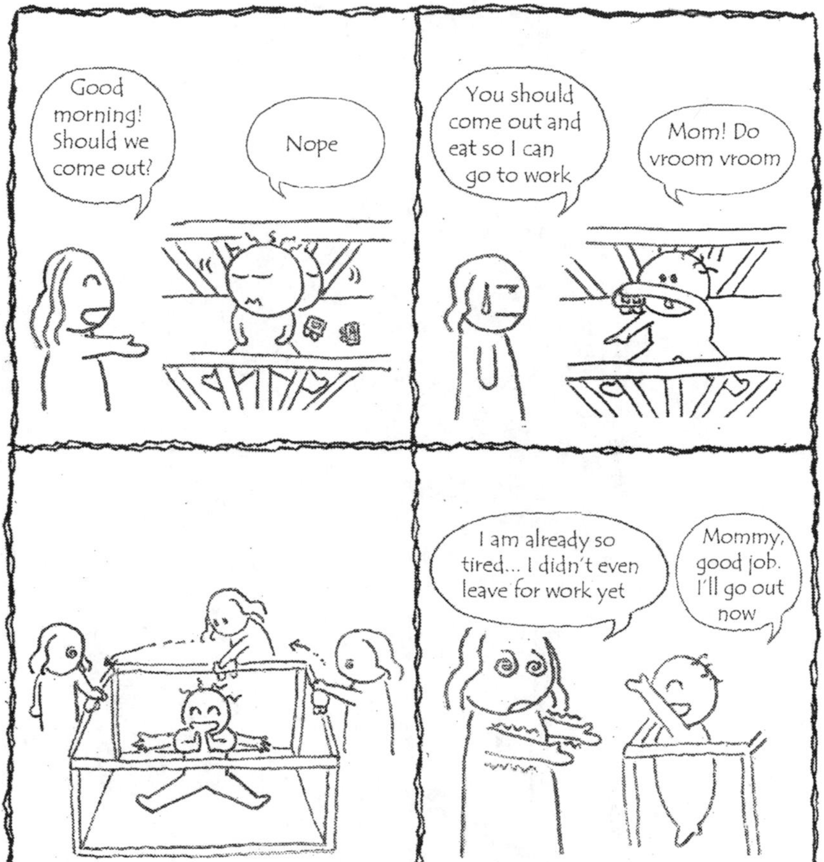
Good morning! Should we come out?
Nope
You should come out and eat so I can go to work
Mom! Do vroom vroom
I am already so tired... I didn't even leave for work yet
Mommy, good job. I'll go out now

DROOL CATCHER

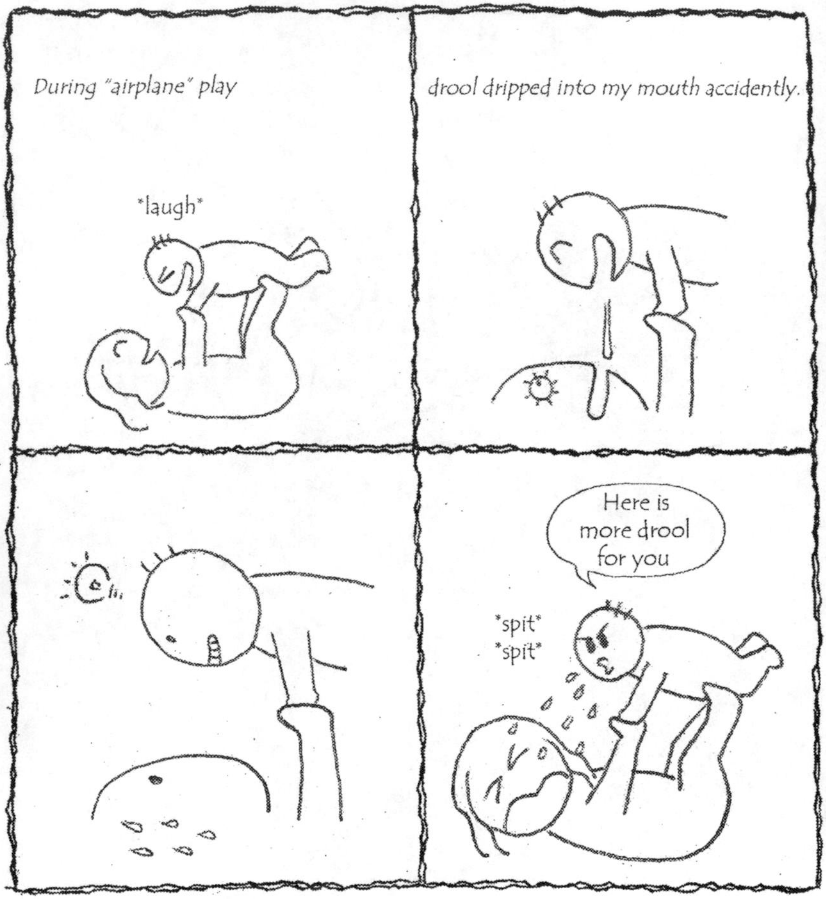
During "airplane" play
laugh
drool dripped into my mouth accidently.
Here is more drool for you
spit
spit

HE'S A SMART FELLA

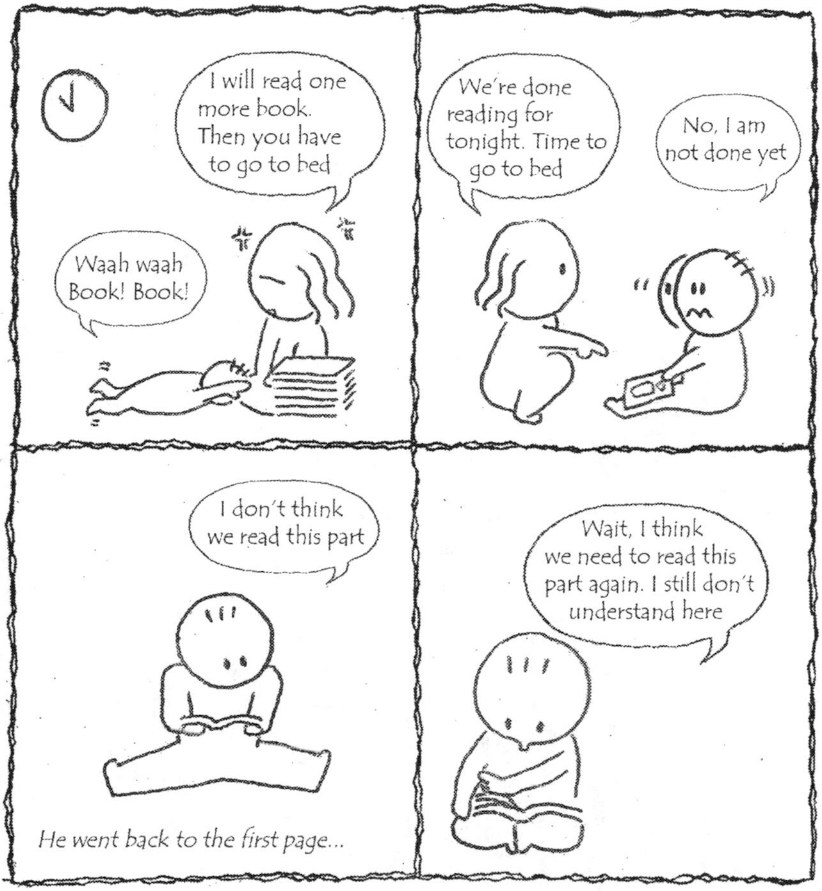

I will read one more book. Then you have to go to bed
Waah waah Book! Book!
We're done reading for tonight. Time to go to bed
No, I am not done yet
I don't think we read this part
He went back to the first page...
Wait, I think we need to read this part again. I still don't understand here

EARLY MORNING ROUTINE

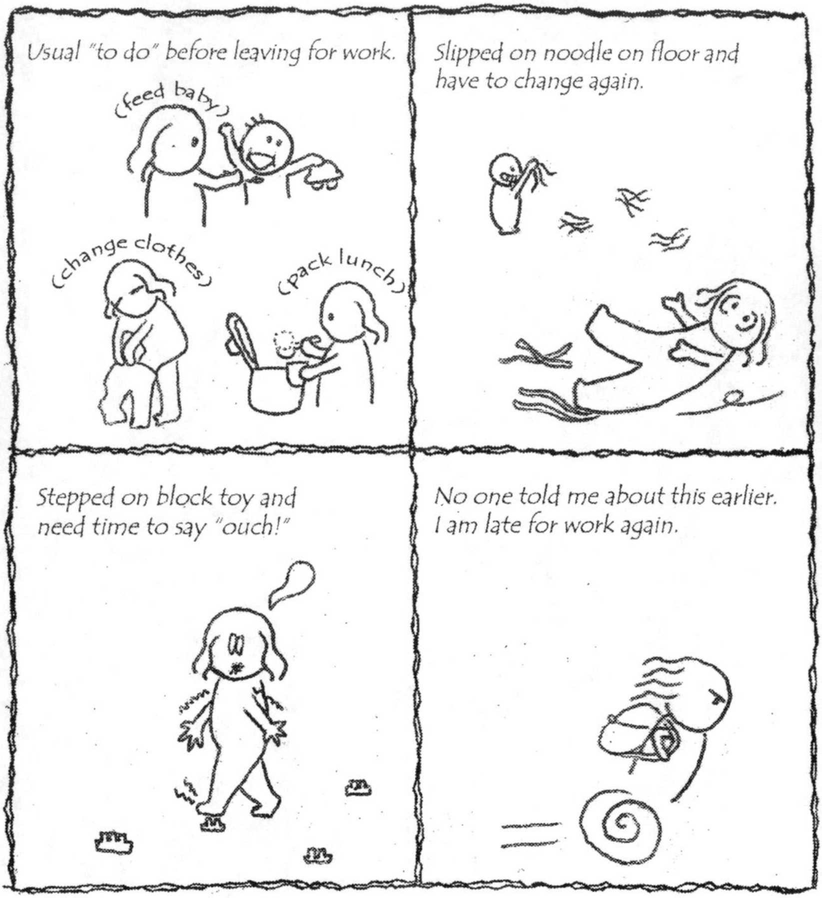
Usual "to do" before leaving for work.
(feed baby)
(change clothes)
(pack lunch)
Slipped on noodle on floor and have to change again.
Stepped on block toy and need time to say "ouch!"
No one told me about this earlier. I am late for work again.

MOM VS. DAD

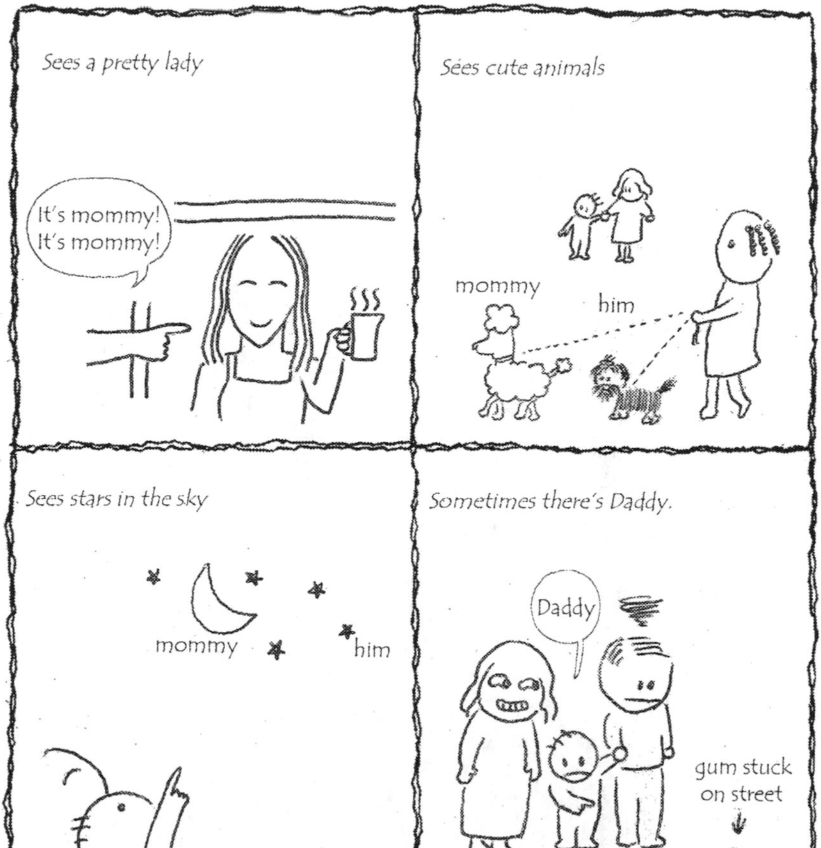

Sees a pretty lady
It's mommy! It's mommy!
Sées cute animals
mommy
him
Sees stars in the sky
mommy
him
Sometimes there's Daddy.
Daddy
gum stuck on street

ENERGIZER

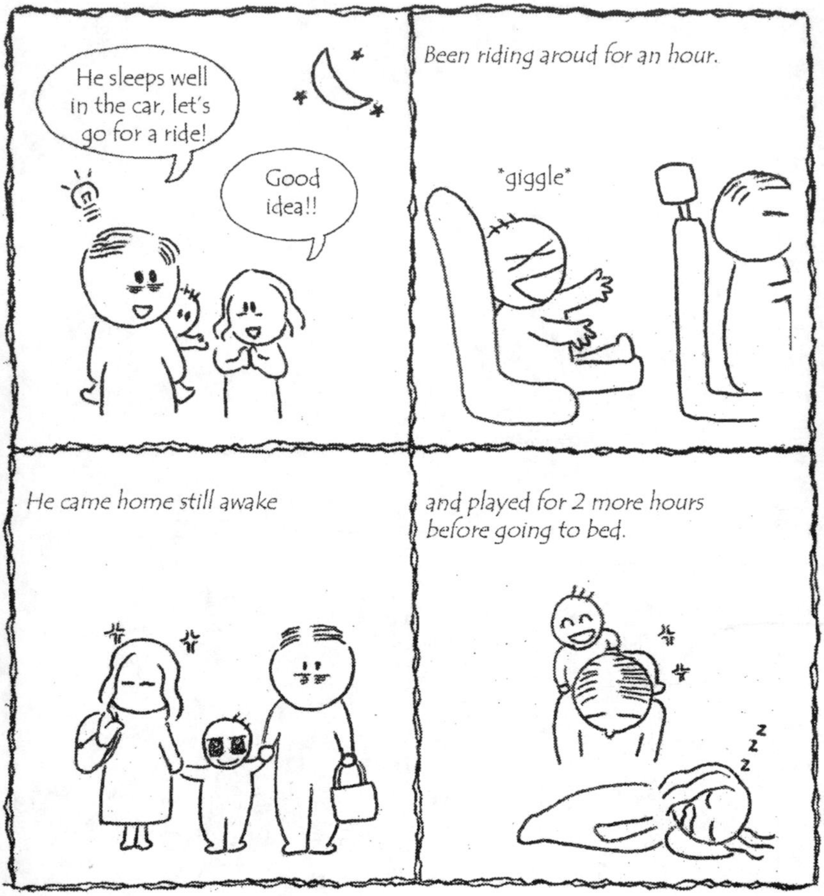
He sleeps well in the car, let's go for a ride!
Good idea!!
Been riding aroud for an hour.
giggle
He came home still awake
and played for 2 more hours before going to bed.
z z z

NAME CREATOR

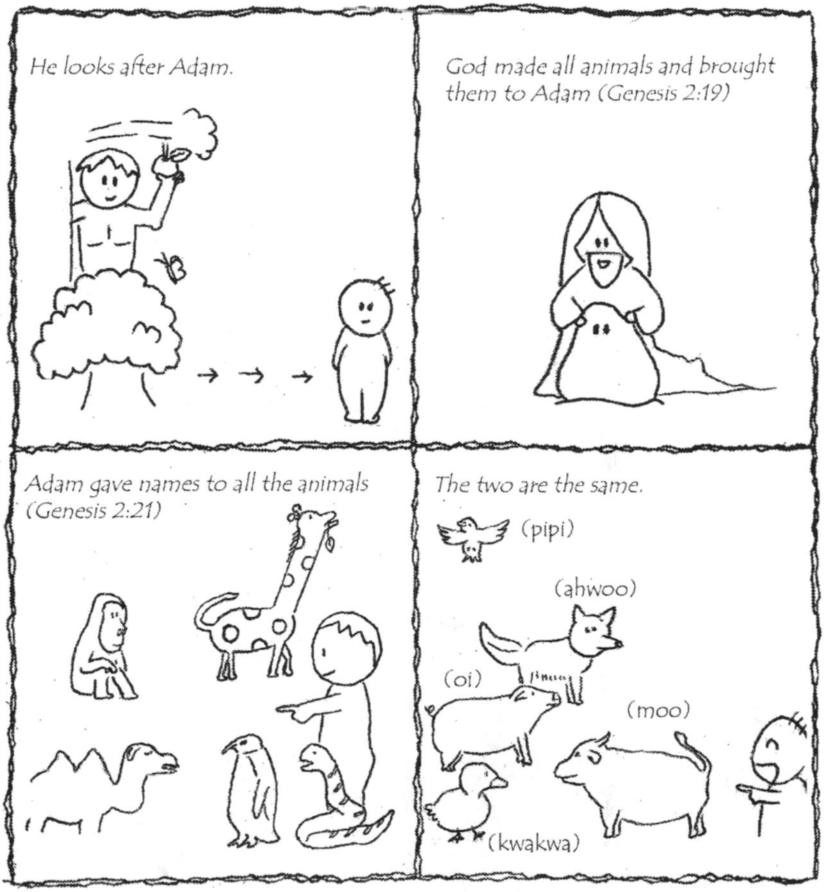
He looks after Adam.
God made all animals and brought them to Adam (Genesis 2:19)
Adam gave names to all the animals (Genesis 2:21)
The two are the same.
(pipi)
(ahwoo)
(oi)
(moo)
(kwakwa)

POTTY TRAINING #1

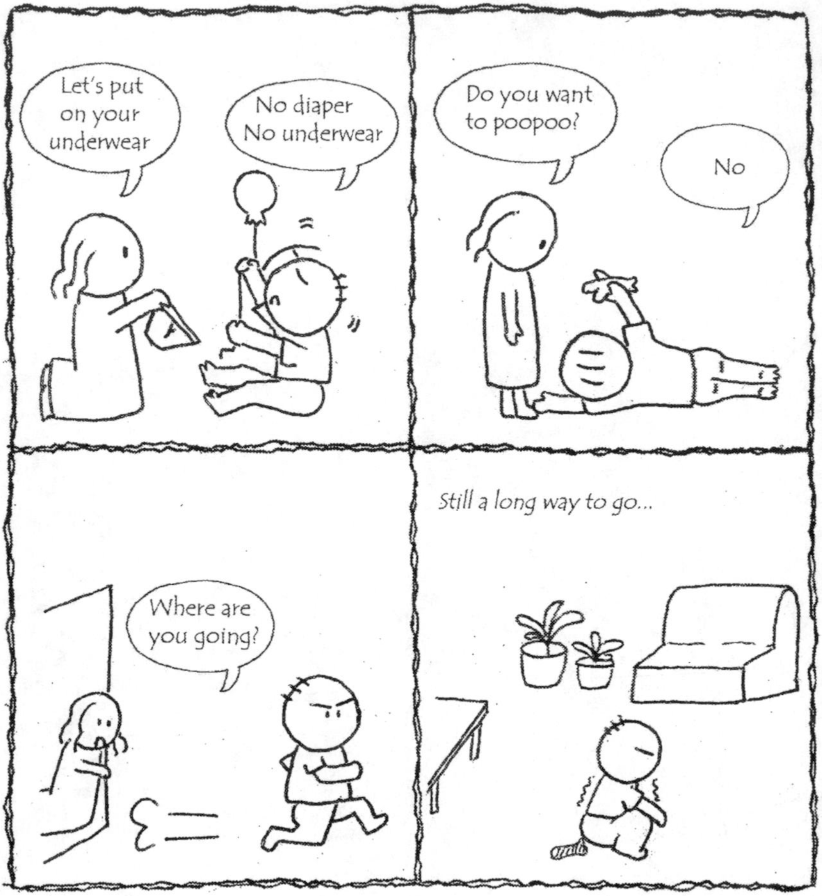

Let's put on your underwear
No diaper No underwear
Do you want to poopoo?
No
Where are you going?
Still a long way to go...

PEE PEE #1

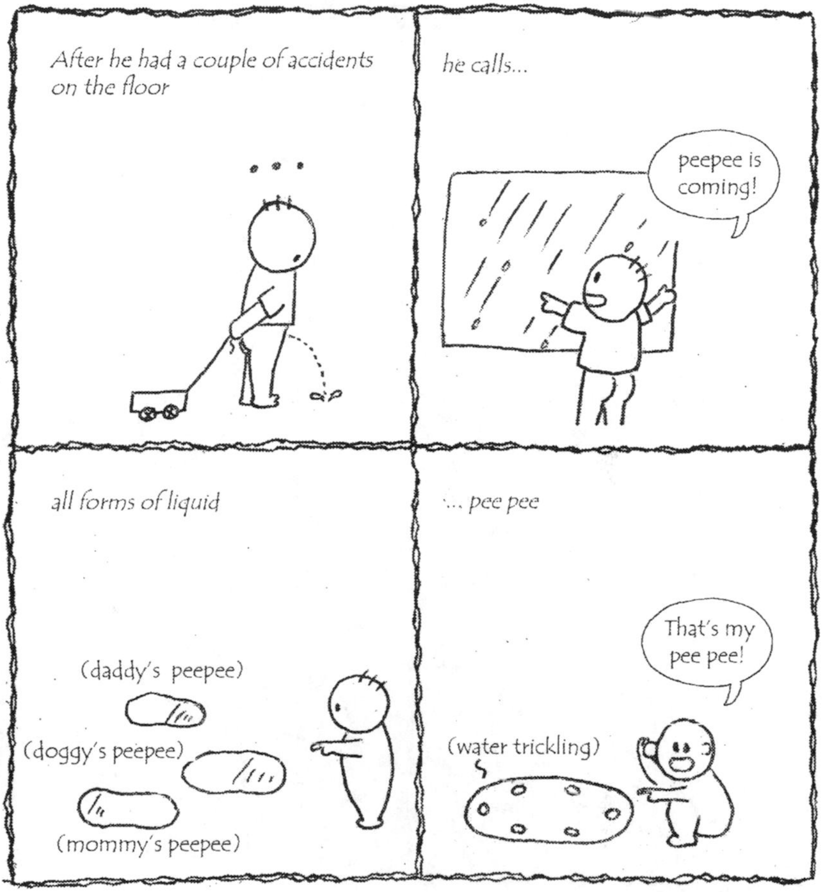

After he had a couple of accidents on the floor
he calls...
peepee is coming!
all forms of liquid
(daddy's peepee)
(doggy's peepee)
(mommy's peepee)
... pee pee
That's my pee pee!
(water trickling)

PEE PEE #2

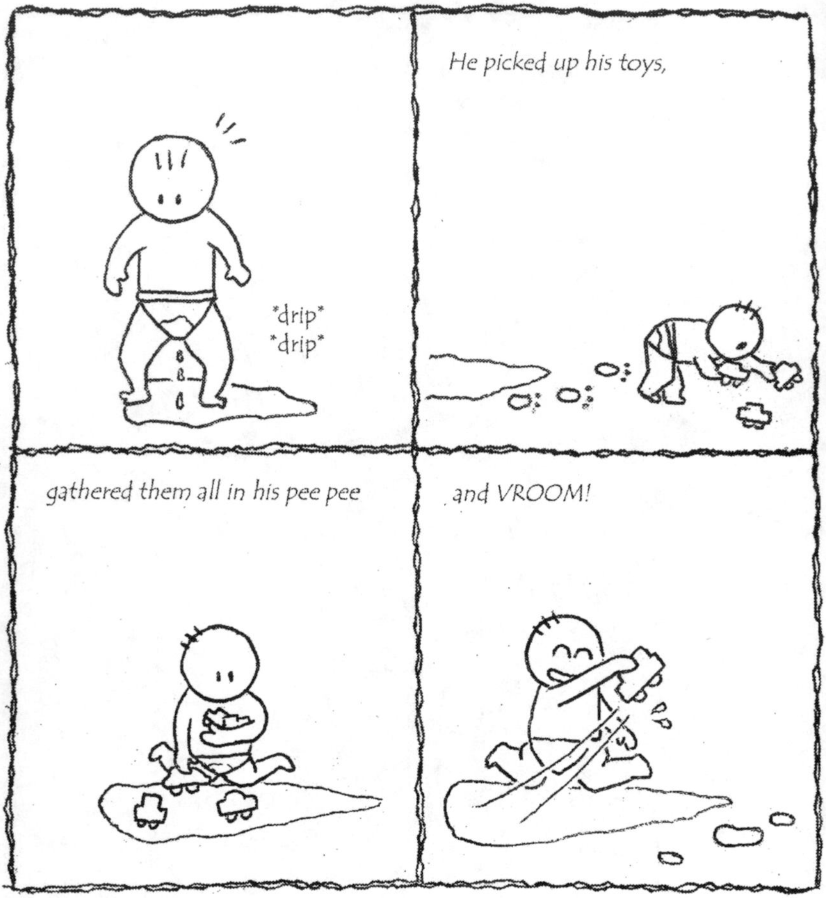
drip
drip
He picked up his toys,
gathered them all in his pee pee
and VROOM!

A SPECIAL GIFT

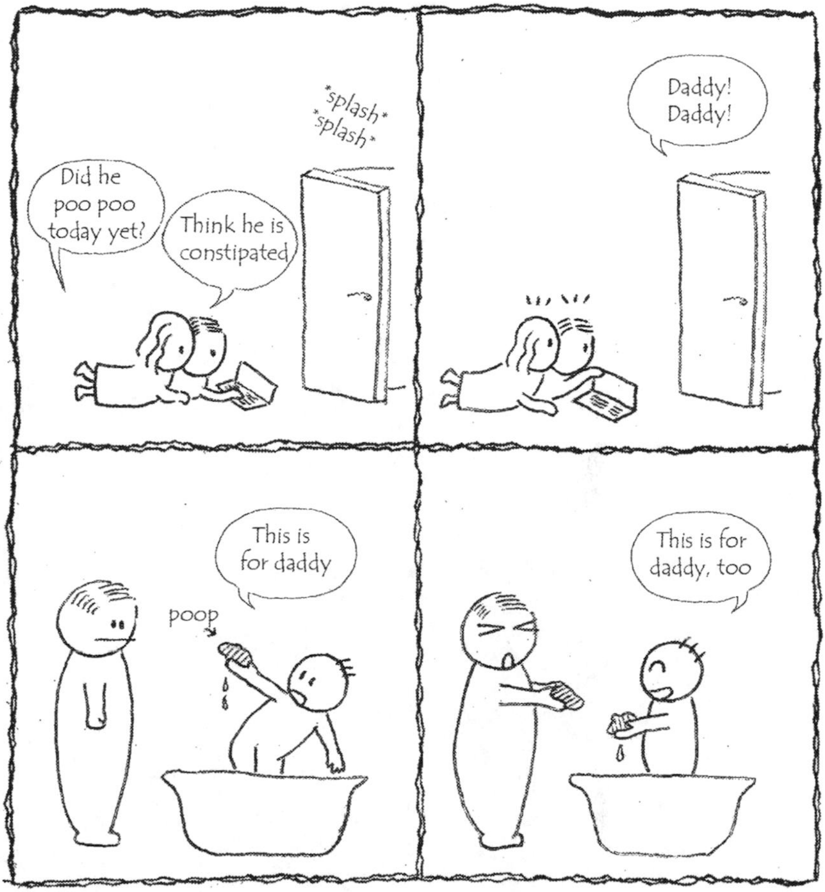
splash
splash
Did he poo poo today yet?
Think he is constipated
Daddy! Daddy!
This is for daddy
poop
This is for daddy, too

MOMMY LIKES SURPRISES

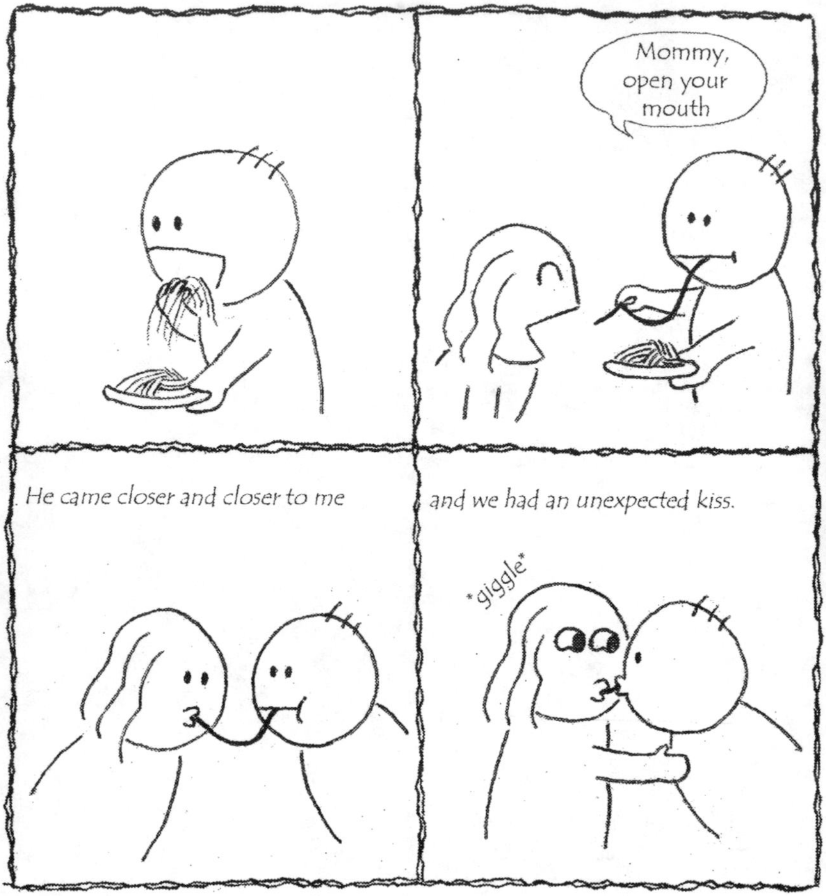
Mommy, open your mouth
He came closer and closer to me
and we had an unexpected kiss.
giggle

FINALLY SUCCESS?

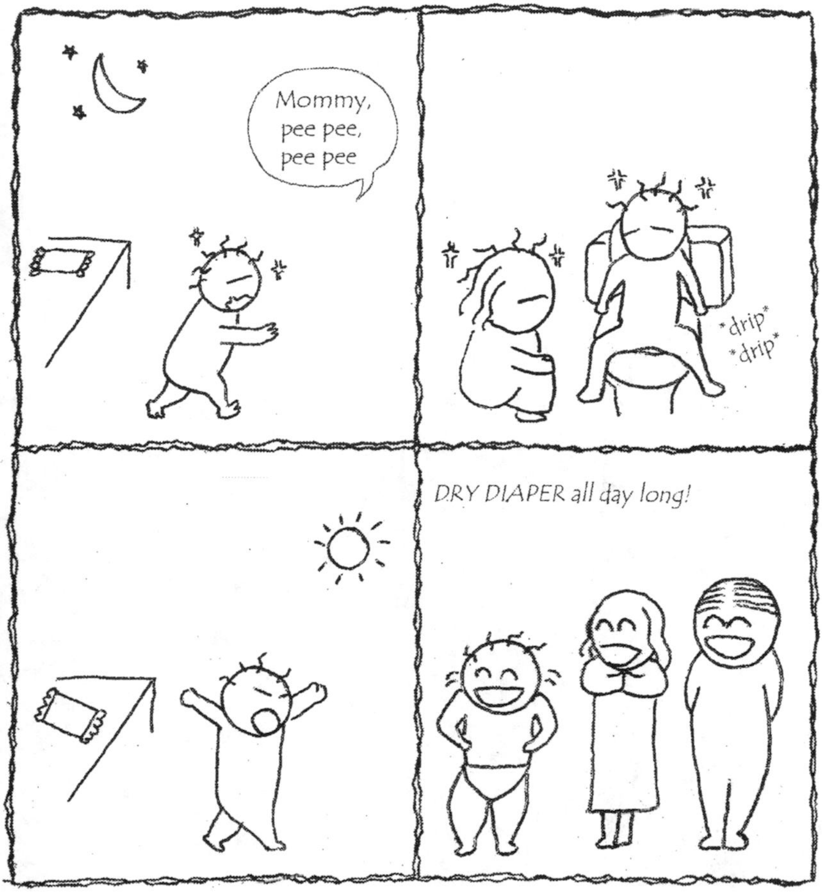
Mommy, pee pee, pee pee
drip *drip*
DRY DIAPER all day long!

MARKING HIS TERRITORY

Doggies mark their territory with their urine.

He marks his territory with his toy cars.

HIS SLEEP PATTERN

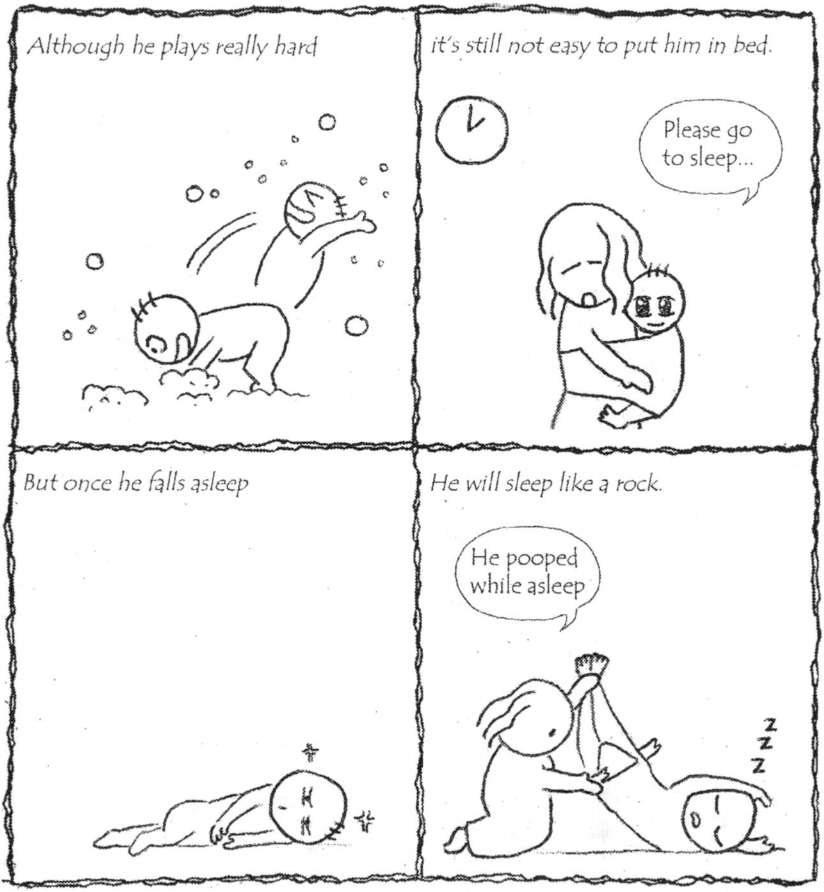
Although he plays really hard
it's still not easy to put him in bed.
Please go to sleep...
But once he falls asleep
He will sleep like a rock.
He pooped while asleep
Z Z Z

FEAR

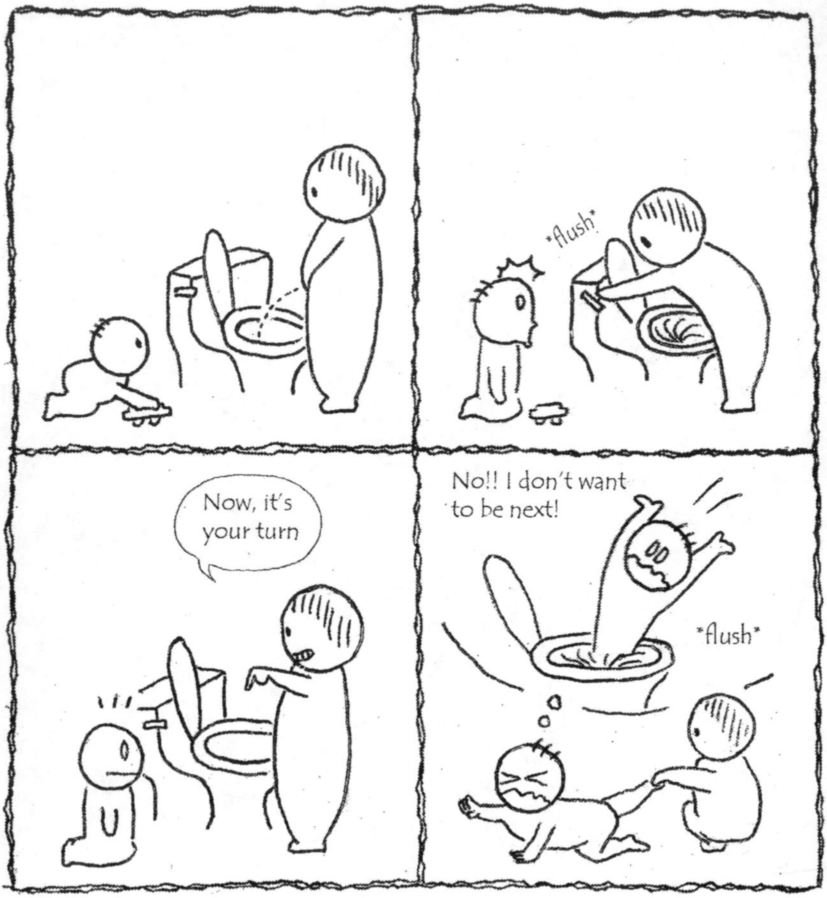
flush
Now, it's your turn
No!! I don't want to be next!
flush

HAPPIEST MOMENT

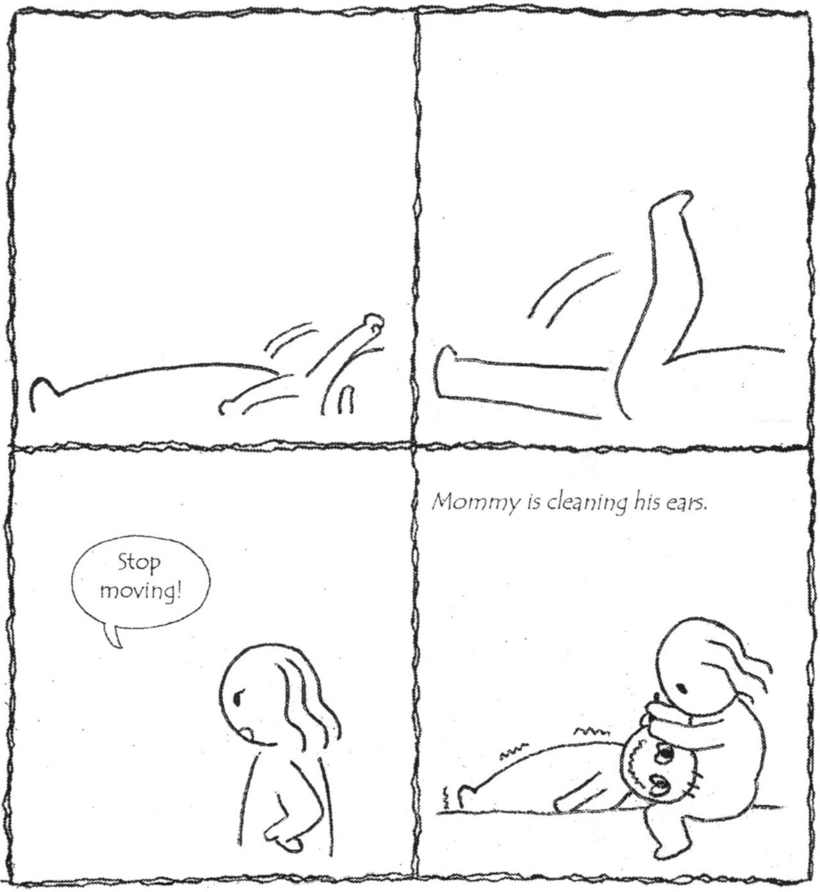

Stop moving!
Mommy is cleaning his ears.

IS THERE A NAME FOR IT?

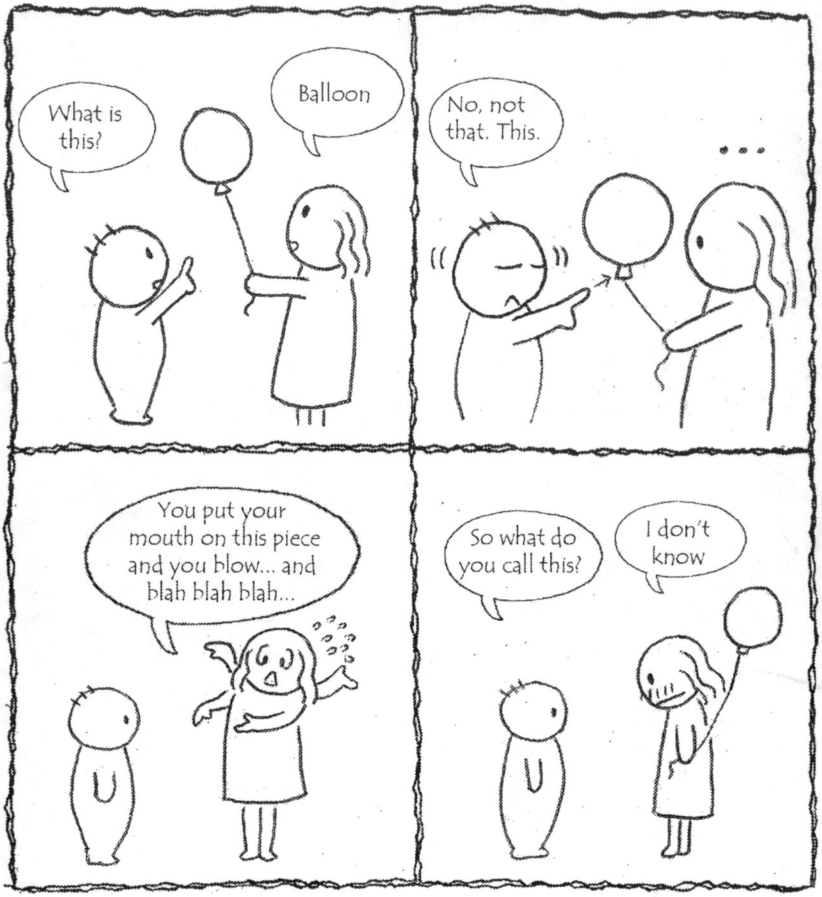
What is this?
Balloon
No, not that. This.
...
You put your mouth on this piece and you blow... and blah blah blah...
So what do you call this?
I don't know

CAN'T GET ENOUGH

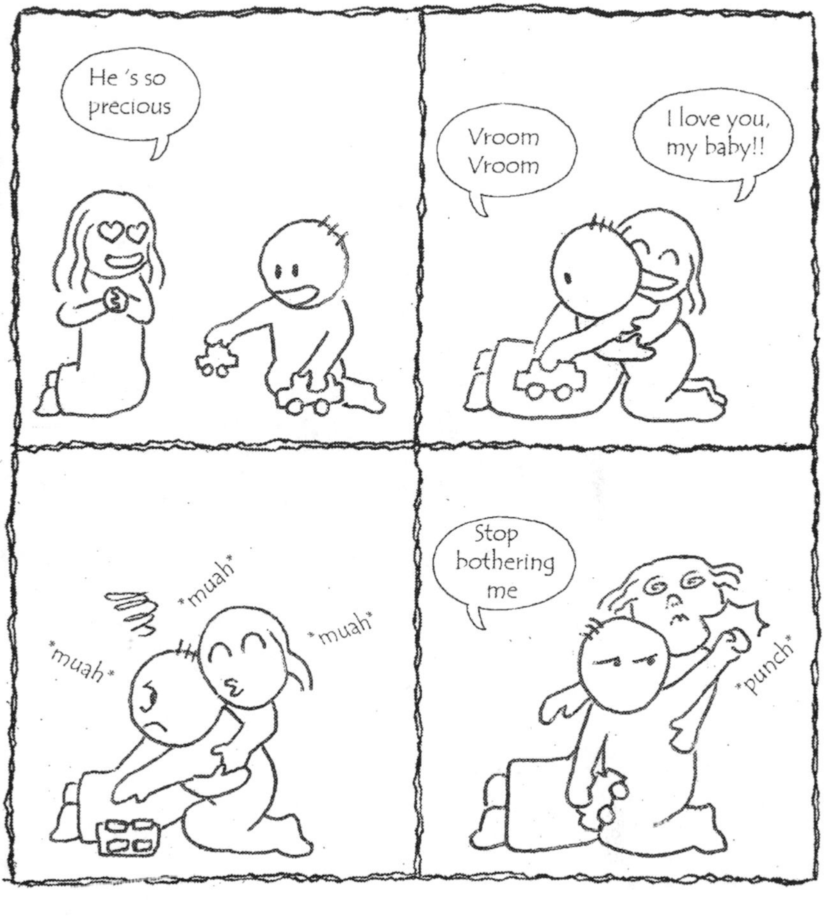
He 's so precious
Vroom Vroom
I love you, my baby!!
muah
muah
muah
Stop bothering me
punch

SO CUTE, SO TASTY

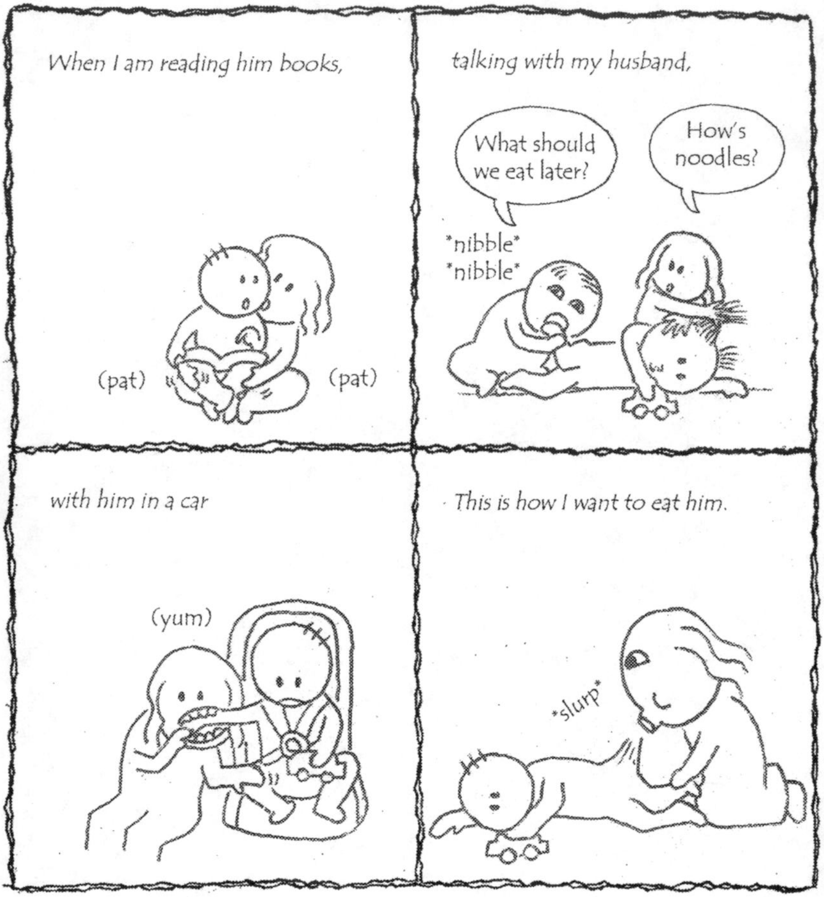
When I am reading him books,
(pat)
(pat)
talking with my husband,
What should we eat later?
How's noodles?
nibble
nibble
with him in a car
(yum)
This is how I want to eat him.
slurp

FORESIGHT

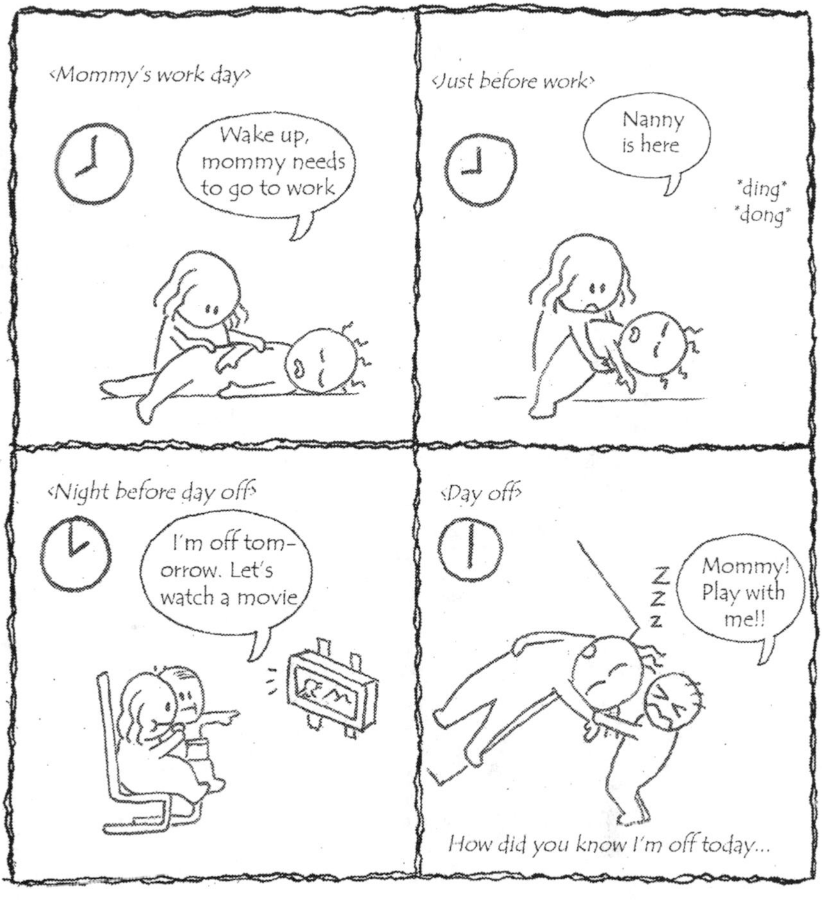
‹Mommy's work day›
Wake up, mommy needs to go to work
‹Just before work›
Nanny is here
ding *dong*
‹Night before day off›
I'm off tom-orrow. Let's watch a movie
‹Day off›
Z Z Z
Mommy! Play with me!!
How did you know I'm off today...

GRILLED FISH

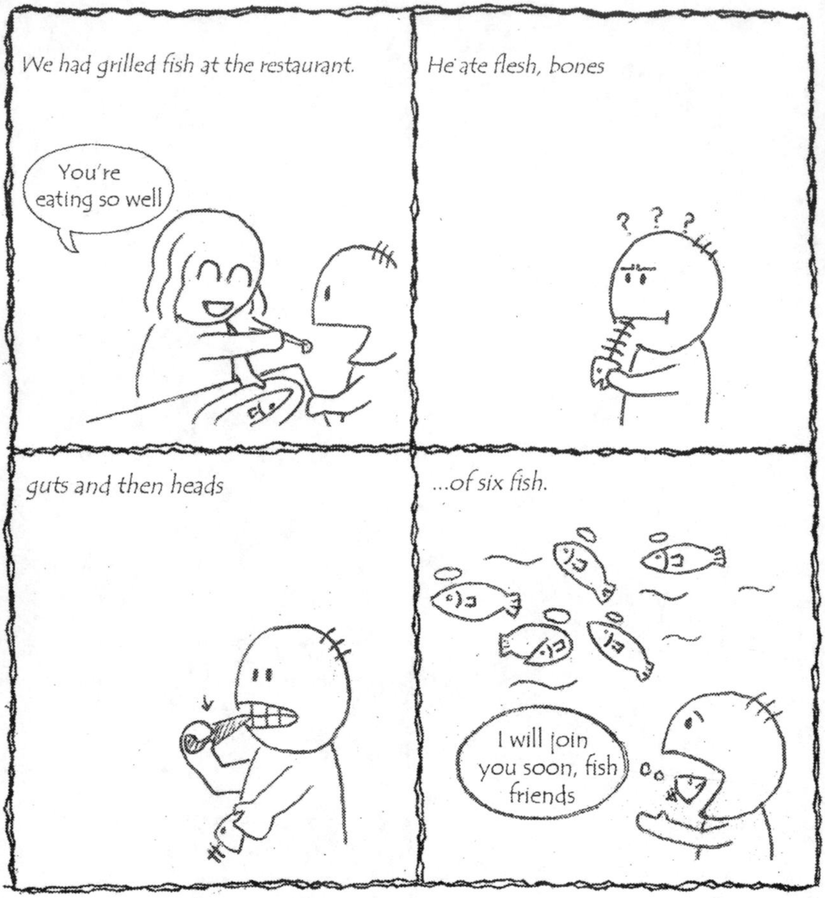
We had grilled fish at the restaurant.
You're eating so well
He ate flesh, bones
? ? ?
guts and then heads
...of six fish.
I will join you soon, fish friends

PERSONIFICATION

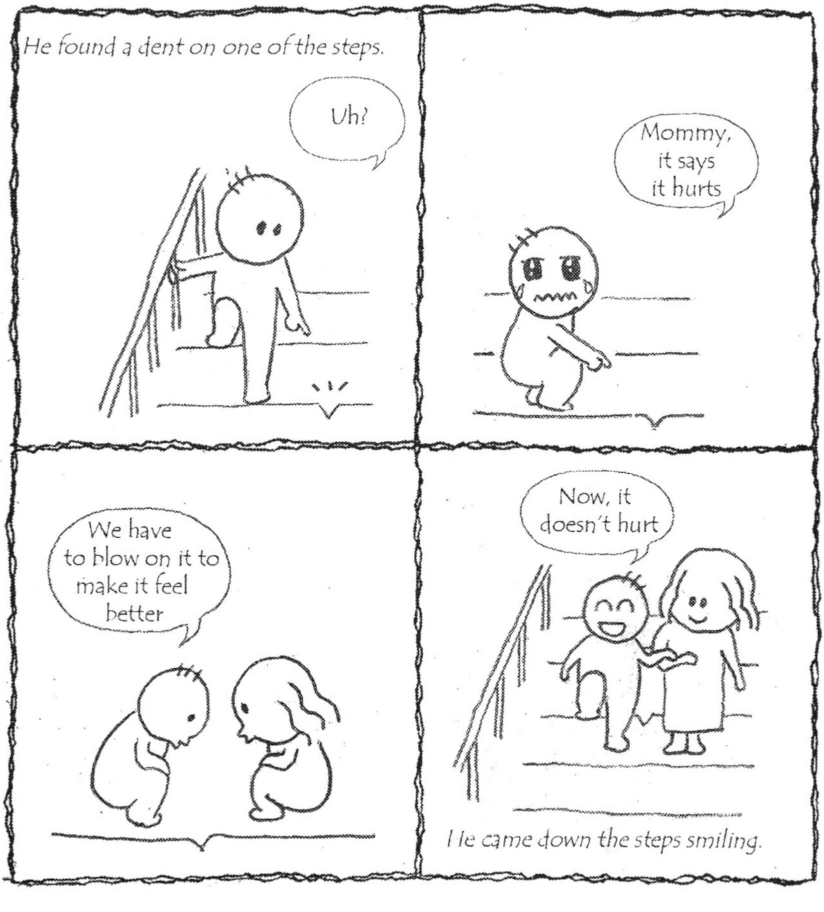
He found a dent on one of the steps.
Uh?
Mommy, it says it hurts
We have to blow on it to make it feel better
Now, it doesn't hurt
He came down the steps smiling.

STUCK ON ME #1

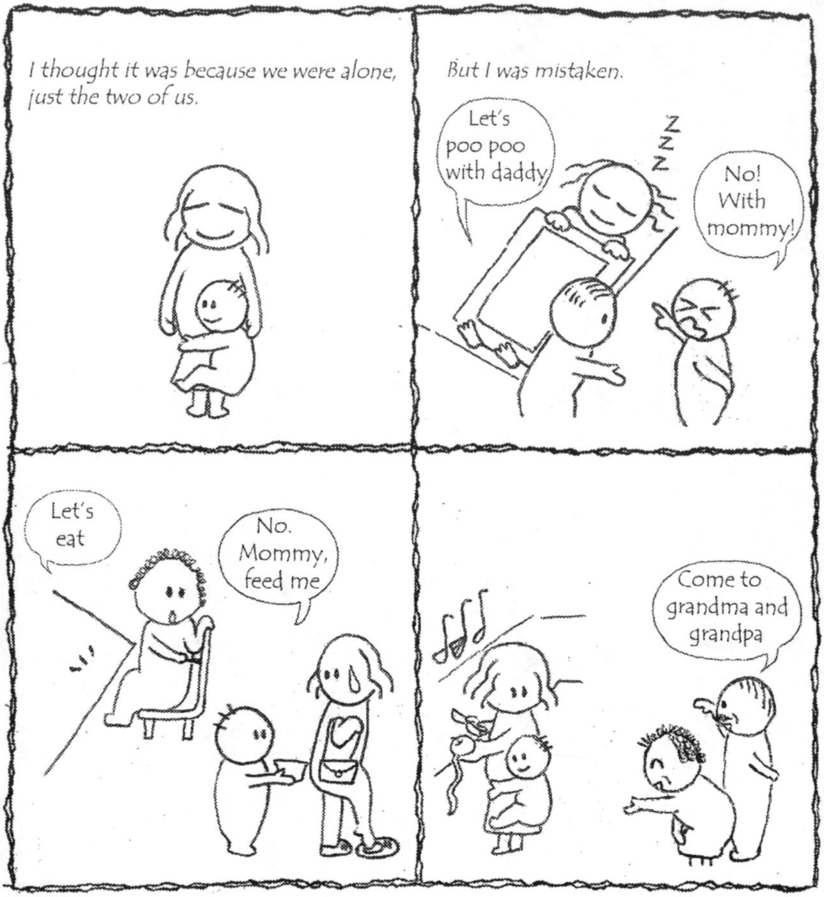
I thought it was because we were alone, just the two of us.
But I was mistaken.
Let's poo poo with daddy
Z Z Z
No! With mommy!
Let's eat
No. Mommy, feed me
Come to grandma and grandpa

STUCK ON ME #2

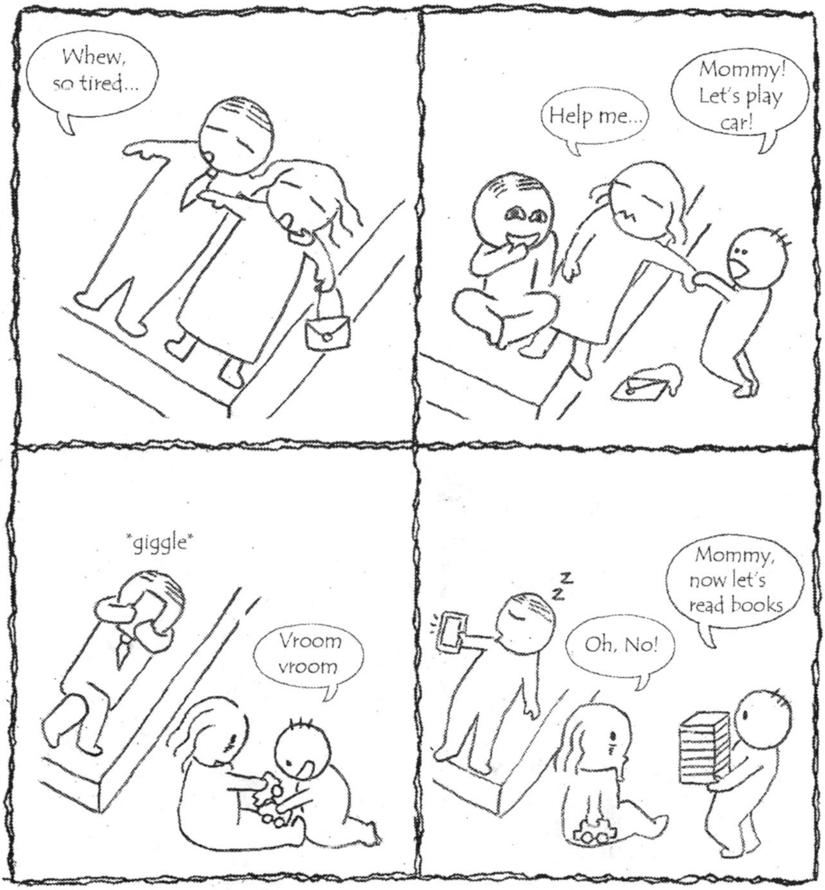

Whew, so tired...
Help me...
Mommy! Let's play car!
giggle
Vroom vroom
Mommy, now let's read books
Oh, No!

REASSIGNED RESPONSIBILITIES

NOTHING CAN BE HIDDEN FROM YOU

DUAL PERSONALITY

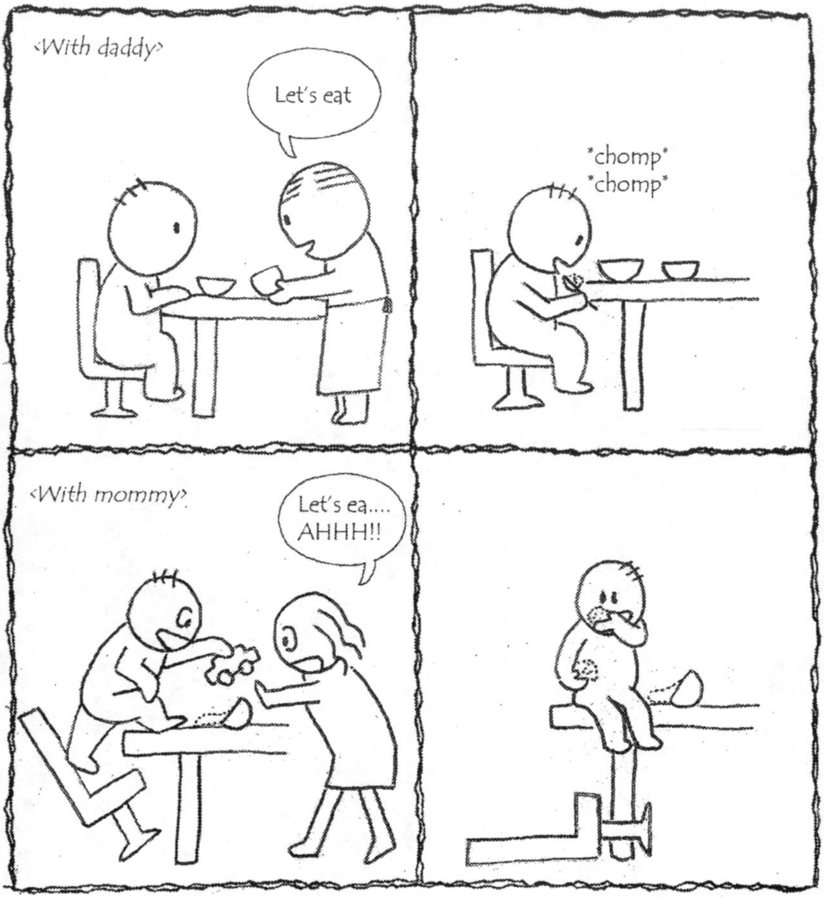
‹With daddy›
Let's eat
chomp
chomp
‹With mommy›
Let's ea....
AHHH!!

PLAY WITH ME

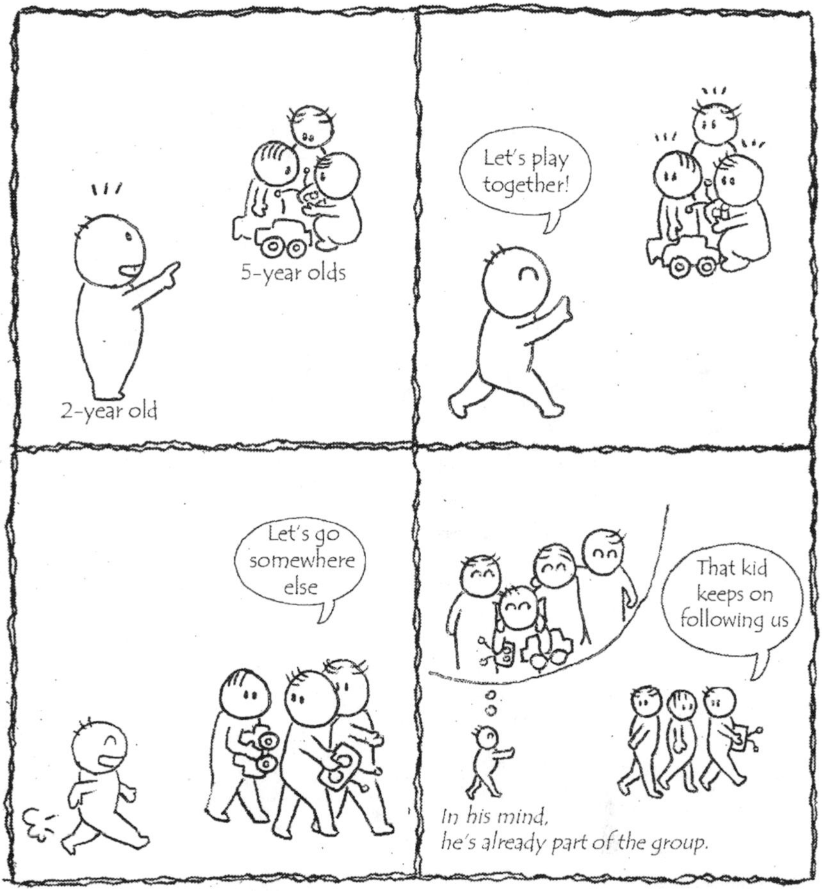
5-year olds
2-year old
Let's play together!
Let's go somewhere else
That kid keeps on following us
In his mind,
he's already part of the group.

UNREASONABLE PERMISSION

MEALTIME PRAYER

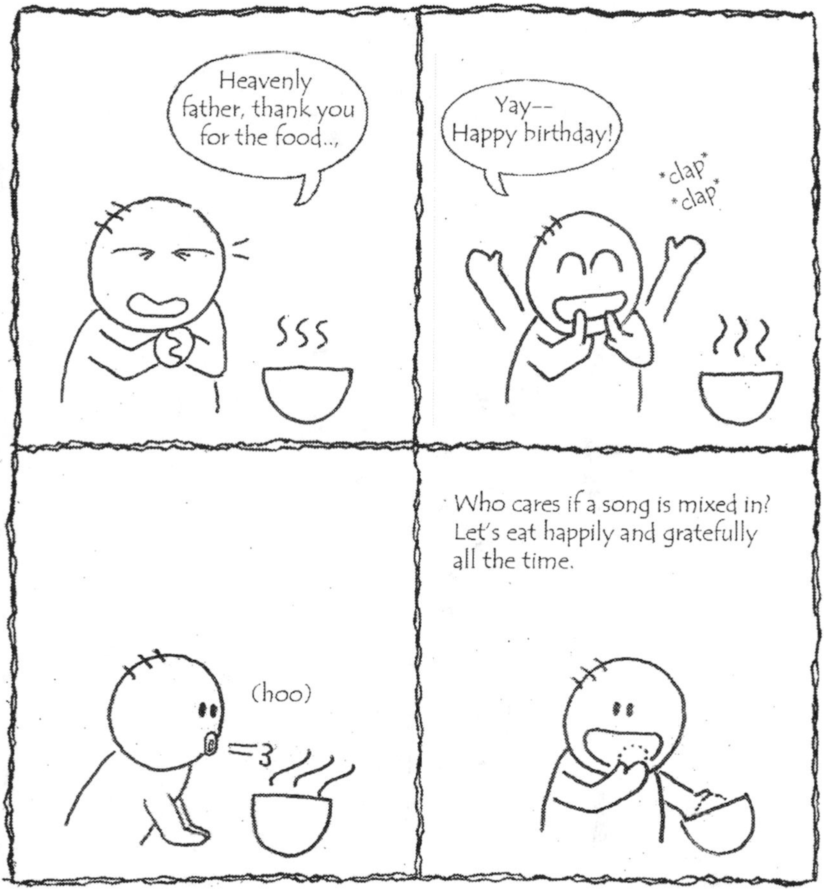
Heavenly father, thank you for the food..,
Yay-- Happy birthday!
clap *clap*
(hoo)
Who cares if a song is mixed in? Let's eat happily and gratefully all the time.

SHARING

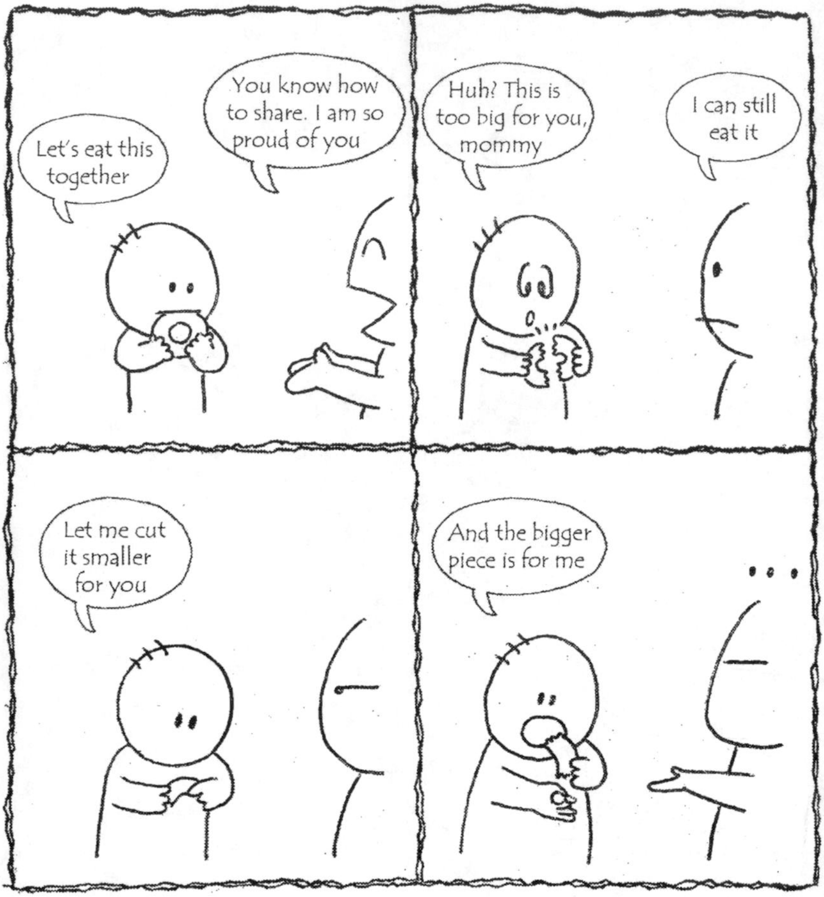
Let's eat this together
You know how to share. I am so proud of you
Huh? This is too big for you, mommy
I can still eat it
Let me cut it smaller for you
And the bigger piece is for me
. . .

SHOW AND TELL

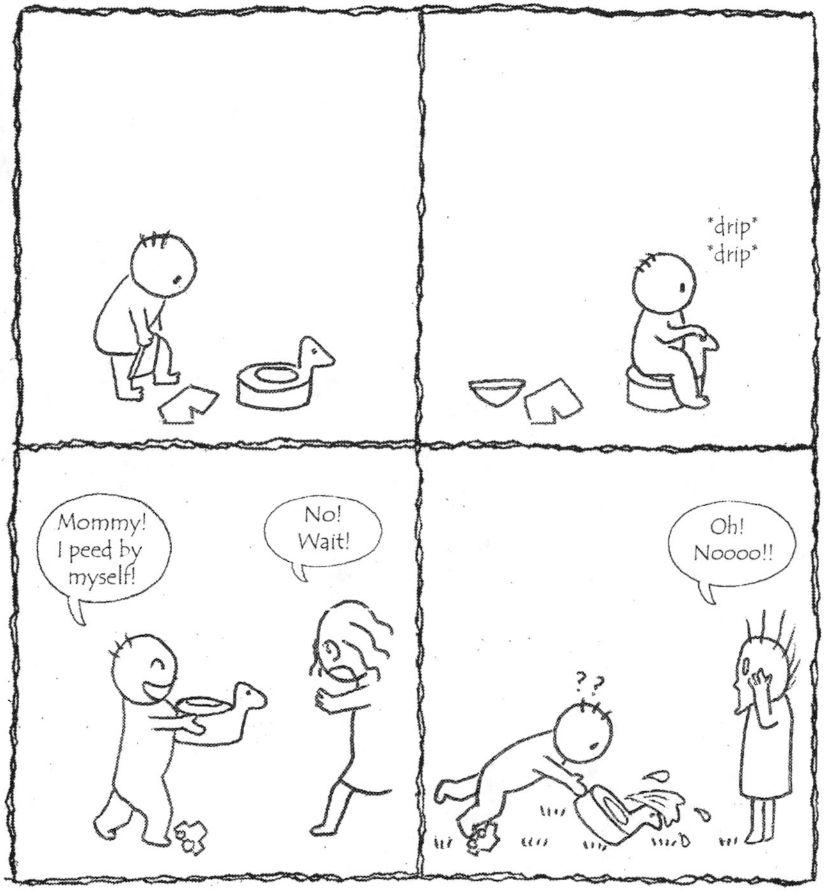
drip
drip
Mommy! I peed by myself!
No! Wait!
Oh! Noooo!!

SHIFTING ATTENTION

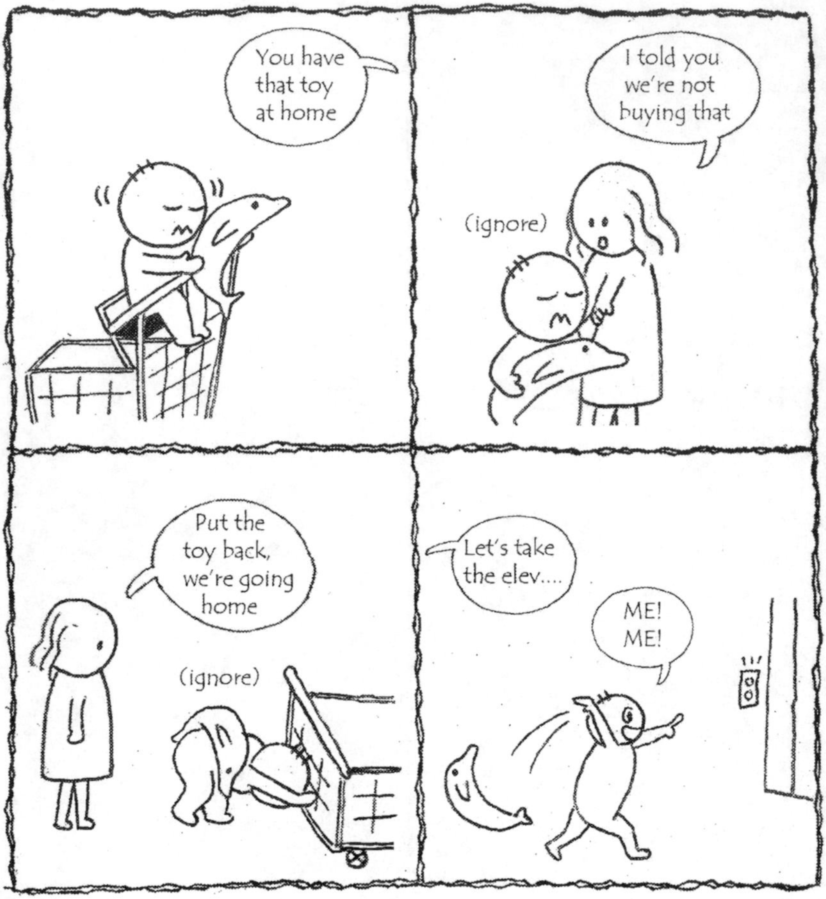
You have that toy at home
I told you we're not buying that
(ignore)
Put the toy back, we're going home
(ignore)
Let's take the elev....
ME! ME!

LIKE FATHER, LIKE SON

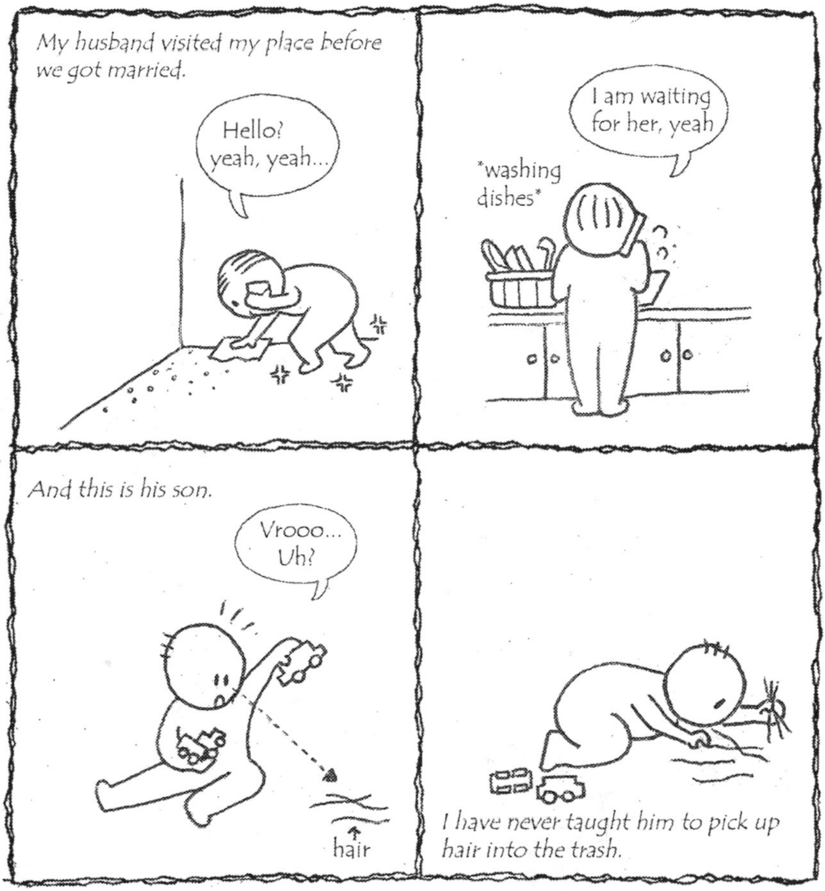
My husband visited my place before we got married.
Hello? yeah, yeah...
I am waiting for her, yeah
washing dishes
And this is his son.
Vrooo... Uh?
hair
I have never taught him to pick up hair into the trash.

AMBIDEXTROUS

I am right-handed.

My right leg is his designated chair.

It is not easy to pick up food because of him.

Things change so I need to change, too. I am now ambidextrous.

HOLIDAY

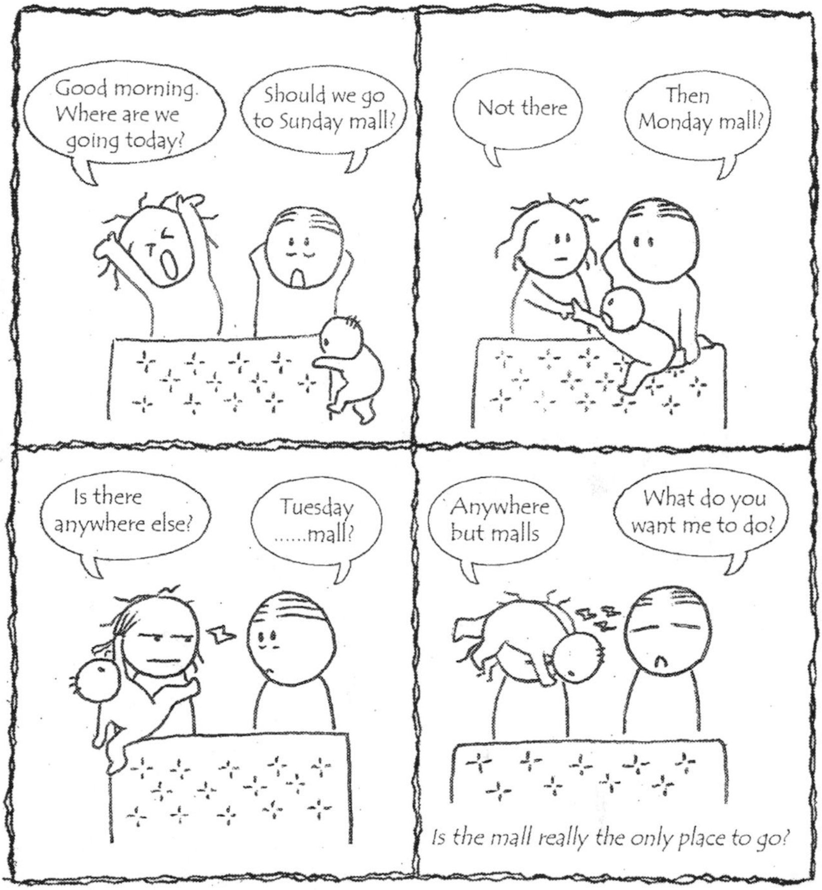
Good morning. Where are we going today?
Should we go to Sunday mall?
Not there
Then Monday mall?
Is there anywhere else?
Tuesday ......mall?
Anywhere but malls
What do you want me to do?
Is the mall really the only place to go?

COMPLIMENTS #2

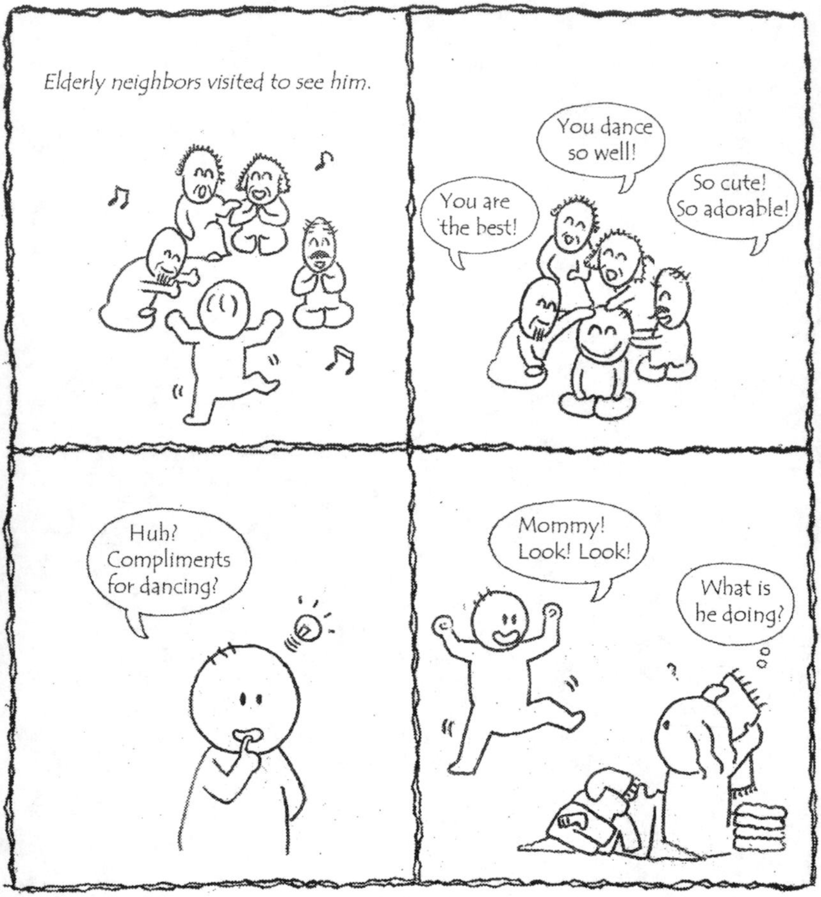

Elderly neighbors visited to see him.
You dance so well!
You are the best!
So cute! So adorable!
Huh? Compliments for dancing?
Mommy! Look! Look!
What is he doing?

THE SANDMAN COMETH

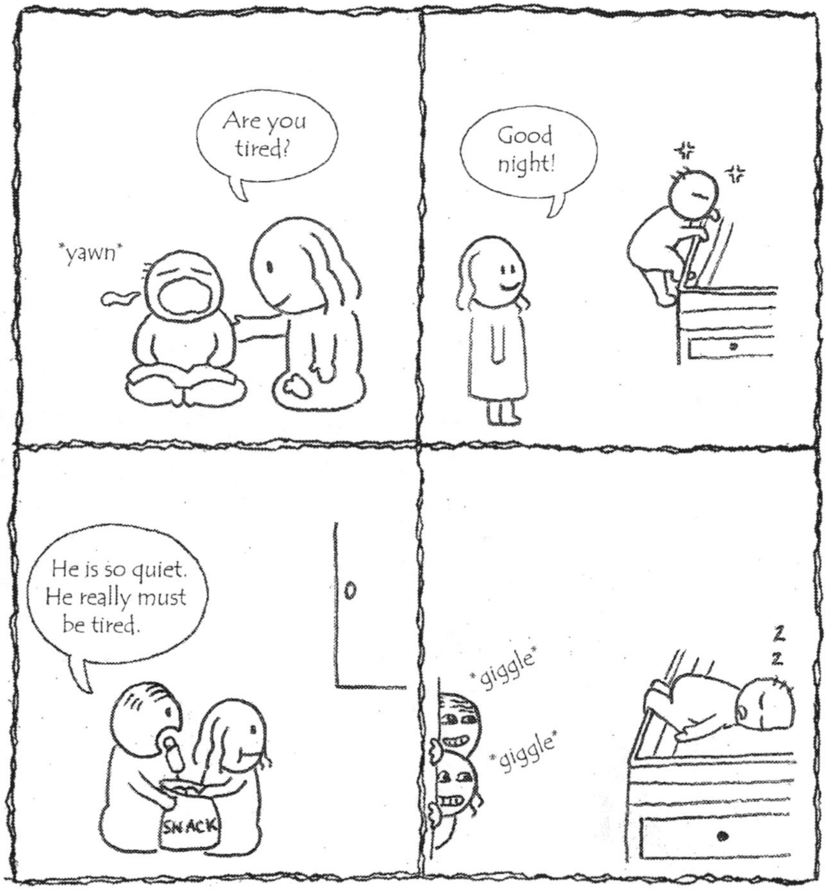
Are you tired?
yawn
Good night!
He is so quiet. He really must be tired.
SNACK
giggle
giggle
z z

ABOUT THE AUTHOR

Yul Kim is an operating room (OR) nurse at a university hospital in the New York City area. It has been her dream to be an OR nurse, and she enjoys living out her dream. Since her son was born in 2014, she has been fully emerged in the joys of motherhood. As a full-time nurse, wife, and mom, her life has been full of busyness, but she enjoys the challenges thrown at her every day while still pioneering her new tomorrow.

Printed in the United States
By Bookmasters